D1715335

PRAISE FOR *THE FRESHMAN YEAR AT AN HBCU*

"The Freshman Year at an HBCU is a much needed book for young people that attend HBCUs. If I could, I would provide this book for each freshman that walks through our doors. This book could help in the area of retention. It is a blessing and so needed."

—***Elizabeth Spraggins***, Retention Specialist, Miles College

"The Freshman Year at an HBCU provides insight into the myriad of complex challenges faced by today's college freshmen from diverse backgrounds. For those students experiencing college with little or no knowledge of the varied experiences/expectations they will face, this book serves as a wonderful tool."

—**Ontario Wooden**, Dean of University College, North Carolina Central University

"Kelly DeLong records the lives of four freshman students at a historically black college and university, and I know of no other scholar who has shown interest in the subject and covered it with such grace and compassion. Although he documents their stresses and strains, unpredictable and fun moments, DeLong is also instructive: freshman students should understand the intellectual demands of college, learn from each other, and remain focused."

—**James A. Hefner**, former president of Tennessee State University and Jackson State University

The Freshman Year at an HBCU

The Freshman Year at an HBCU

Kelly DeLong

Owl Canyon Press

First Edition, 2015

Library of Congress Cataloging-in-Publication Data

DeLong, Kelly.
The Freshman Year at an HBCU—1st ed.
p. cm.
ISBN: 978-0-9911211-5-1
2014956780
Owl Canyon Press
Boulder, Colorado

 All student names have been changed to protect their identity.

I need to give thanks to all the many people I interviewed for this book, especially Tameka, Ashley, Michael and Reggie, who dutifully came to my office weekly just so I could barrage them with questions.

Thanks to Susan Wright and Rene´ Saldaña, Jr. for their advice and encouragement. Thanks also goes to Shirley Williams-Kirksey, who, without knowing it, challenged me to write this book. Finally, I thank my students who read portions of this work and gave me feedback, and, also, I need to thank Tikenya Foster-Singletary, Kimberly Payne, Lakeitha Wilson and Robert Edwards for helping prepare the manuscript.

Contents

For my students—past, present, future

Introduction

Every August they come—thousands of them—wide-eyed, excited, eager freshmen ready to take on this new adventure called *College*. They come from California, Texas, New York, Michigan, Missouri, Georgia, the Caribbean, Africa—they come from nearly everywhere. They've saved, they've borrowed, they've won scholarships to attend college. Their families have hugged them good-bye, have told them they are proud and have cried as they drove away. That first week these freshmen walk around in groups, with roommates, with just-met friends, taking in their new surroundings, acclimating themselves to a new city, to new buildings, to their new home. They walk around giddy, laughing, smiling at the thought that they are finally in college—finally!—that they are new adults with new freedoms and new responsibilities and that in the not-too-distant future—if they can successfully manage their new freedoms and responsibilities—they will hold in their hands their very own college diploma; they will be a college graduate. But, first, they have to tackle the toughest of all the college years—the freshman year.

There is nothing in college that compares with the freshman year. It is the year in which students discover what they are made of. Most first-time college students have never been away from home before, away from their neighborhoods, from their own bedrooms, from Mom's cooking. Now for the first time in their lives they have to cope without their families by their side, and for the first time they have to make daily decisions that in the past had been made by Mom or Dad. At first this new life can seem exciting, but it can also prove overwhelming, sometimes even paralyzing.

At the same time freshmen have to adjust to life away from home, they also have to adjust to the college classroom. They will soon discover that college is not high school. College will require much more of them than high school ever did. They will discover that professors will not tolerate excuses and will have higher expectations than their teachers in high school. Freshmen will discover that they will have little time to fall behind and even less to catch up. Semesters move fast in college, and only those who are up to the challenge move on.

Besides adjusting to college life, dealing with homesickness, and the challenges of the classroom, freshmen also have to learn how to manage their social time. They have to choose their friends wisely, work with roommates they more than likely hardly know and have to decide what organizations and clubs and activities best suit them as students and as individuals. Freshmen learn that a poor decision in this area could have far-reaching consequences in their quest for an education.

Students who successfully manage the pitfalls and difficulties of their freshman year will more likely be better suited for the rigors of college that lie ahead. They have a much better chance of graduating. Many students, however, don't make it through their freshman year. At some point, something happens along the way that causes them to leave school. No one benefits when that happens. How can this event—the dropping out of college—be prevented? Is there something that incoming freshmen can learn from to make sure that they are more prepared for college than they might otherwise be and that will quite possibly keep them from leaving school?

The answer is yes. This book tells the story of four college freshmen at a Historically Black College or University (HBCU). It follows them from their first week of college right through their entire freshman year. Along the way the reader will learn about who these four students are as people and as students, what their goals are, what motivates them, and, most importantly, the reader will be with them through their difficulties and their mistakes, as well as their triumphs. The reader will learn, through the story of these freshmen, what to do and what not to do. The reader will learn what it takes to survive the freshman year.

The Freshmen

To find freshmen who were willing to let me interview them during their first year of college, I spoke to four classes of freshman English. One freshman from each of these classes volunteered, two females and two males. They agreed to stop by my office once a week in order for me to ask them questions so I could learn about them and their lives as students. Here are those four freshmen and here is what I learned about them.

Tameka

Tameka was the first to volunteer. Though she looked unsure of herself while she sat across from me in my office, the way she answered my questions led me to believe that she is a determined young woman. She knows what she wants. The oldest of three raised by a single mother in rural Virginia, Tameka believes, she says, "in never looking for a handout and never depending on someone else to give me what I want." She learned these lessons from her mother, a customer service representative for several churches. Tameka's father has played next to no role in her life. In the last several years she has only seen him on three occasions. It has always been her hardworking mother who has guided and pushed her to achieve all that she is capable of achieving.

Tameka's goal after graduating with a B.S. in Biology is to go to dental school. She says, "I always wanted to be a doctor, but never wanted to be part of making life-and-death decisions." She chose dentistry as her profession of choice after a talk with her mother's dentist, who explained to her that African Americans are underrepresented in the field. "He told me how blacks often have been discouraged from becoming dentists, how he had been told that he wouldn't be able to cut it in college and that he would never be a dentist," she says. Angered by this discouragement, he set out to prove the naysayers wrong. His story of perseverance inspired Tameka to become a dentist. (And, too, she says, "I like that they make good money.")

A very good student in high school, Tameka believes she is ready for the rigors of college. Besides achieving a 3.89 G.P.A. in high school, ranking 14th out of her class of 230, Tameka also logged thirty to thirty-five hours a week as a cashier in a restaurant her senior year. On top of that, she took five college courses (including both sections of College Composition) through the local community college. Her schedule in high school proved so exhausting that sleep was hard to come by. She says that she "slept here and there throughout the day." When I ask her why she pushes herself as hard as she does, she replies, "I don't want to be another statistic. And I want to show my brother and my sister that they can make it too."

While she believes she is ready for her freshman year, Tameka has her worries. "I'm worried that my shyness might hold me back," she says. "I'm not someone who wants the spotlight." She's also worried about her proclivity for procrastination. And, as is a concern for so many college students, she says that she worries about money. Funding for her education comes from government loans, a scholarship, her mother and the money she saved from her job. Tameka would like to work while in college and crosses her fingers that she gets a position at Walmart. Despite these worries, Tameka says, "I am a person who is determined, hard-working, smart and driven. I won't let anything hold me back."

When I ask her what grades she expects to achieve her first semester in college, she says, "A in Speech, A in Algebra, A in History, A in Biology, A in Freshman Seminar and probably an A in World Literature."

As the first person in her family to attend college, Tameka says, "I have no plans to mess up this opportunity that I've been given." She's out to prove to herself that she has what it takes to make it, that she is responsible and on her way to becoming a successful adult. Her mother's parting words stick in her mind: "It's your life now. Try to make the best decisions you can."

Michael

Michael, the first male to volunteer, says about himself, "I'm a tall, skinny guy with messed up teeth, but I don't let them bother me anymore. I see them as my trademark. They make me stand out." Indeed, he has a wide gap in his front teeth, but that doesn't stop him from smiling, as he did when he came into my office and said, "I want to be part of your project." He answers questions quickly and has what can only be called "an upbeat personality." Michael is a Mass Media Arts major who would one day like to be a TV personality like his idols Terrence J and Ryan Seacrest. "I want to have my own show dealing with societal and celebrity issues," he says.

Michael grew up in Columbia, South Carolina with his mother and father and three older brothers. Neither of his parents graduated from high school. His father works as a short order cook, while his mother works three jobs: at a printing company, at Subway and at the South Carolina Department of Transportation as a cleaning person. Michael is the first person in his family to go to college right out of high school. The brother closest to Michael in age worked for five years after graduating from high school and has also started his freshman year in college.

The support Michael has received in the pursuit of his education from his family, friends and his church has been, he says, "almost overwhelming. At my high school graduation there were so many people there cheering me on that I cried," he says. He graduated from a predominantly black high school and ranked 48th out of 160 students. While his reported G.P.A. was 3.2, Michael is quick to say that the school made a mistake. "I know my G.P.A. was higher," he says. "It had to be."

Despite the fact that Michael is excited about being a college student, he wasn't always so sure he wanted to go to college. In high school he joined the junior ROTC and had ideas about joining the navy where he could "be on a boat and see the world. I love to travel and I thought that the navy would give me the best opportunity to do that," he says. "My mother encouraged me to join, but on the day I planned on signing my papers, I had a talk with my dad," Michael says. His father steered him towards college. "Besides," Michael says, "by that point I'd already fallen in love with the school and all it had to offer."

Then came the time to find the money to pay for college. His parents hadn't been able to save any money for his schooling. In fact, his father had not been able to work for a while due to an illness. After several grueling and frustrating hours in the financial aid office, Michael discovered that his loans wouldn't cover all the money he needed. He was seven thousand dollars short. He saw his plans slipping away. It didn't look like he would be able to attend the school of his choice. Then a miracle happened. A family friend chipped in and supplied the money needed to fill the gap. Michael would be able to go to school after all.

Michael expects to receive all A's in his classes his first semester. He expects to get a job. (In high school he worked forty-five hours a week.) He expects to get eight hours of sleep a night, and he plans on joining "every club." He says that when it comes to achieving his dreams, "I'm not going to let anything hold me back." When I ask him who or what inspires him, he smiles and says, "I inspire myself."

Ashley

Ashley is a self-described "Daddy's girl." She has two brothers in their mid-twenties, and, so, as the only girl in the family and the youngest child, she says her father "spoils her." If there is something she hasn't done or has put off until the last minute, such as a project for school, her father is always there to help her. And Ashley describes her mother as a friend, as "someone I can talk to about anything." Ashley's parents raised her in the suburbs of Maryland and sent her to a Catholic girls' school that was half black and half white. She has a sleepy look about her eyes. She sits back in her chair with a contentedness students rarely have when sitting in a professor's office for the first time. Ashley seems like the type of person that isn't in a hurry and has few worries.

She grew up in a home where education was stressed. "Both my parents have their Bachelor's degrees, and my oldest brother," she says. Her other brother received an Associate degree in Hotel and Lodging Management from the local community college. "My family is very involved with my schoolwork," she says. "Dad helps me with math and science and Mom with papers," she says. On the occasions her parents weren't home to help her with her homework, her brothers chipped in. Ashley graduated from high school with a 3.3 G.P.A.

Because education was stressed in her house, Ashley would like to be a teacher. Moreover, her cousin, an elementary school teacher, told Ashley about the joys of teaching young children, and this discussion caused Ashley to choose Early Education as her major. Eventually, Ashley says, "I can see myself pursuing higher degrees in education and one day becoming a principal. My parents taught me to aim high and never give up." When she thinks of her parents' advice, she thinks of the way her mother is a fighter who doesn't admit defeat. Her mother recently fell and tore ligaments in her foot and yet fought her injury so that she could get around and do all the things she needed to get done.

When it comes to Ashley's thoughts about college, *fun* is the word that comes to her mind. That's what she expects college to be. She also thinks about "partying all the time." She's aware though that the biggest challenge her first year in college will be staying focused and getting enough sleep. She says, "For me, fun usually comes before work." In high school she had fun and still managed to study four to five hours a night. In college she would like to study as much as she did in high school but hopefully get more sleep than the five to six hours a night she got while in high school.

If there's anything that holds Ashley back, it's that, as she says, "I'm my own worst critic when it comes to grades." Sometimes, she says, she can be a little too hard on herself. And not just where grades are concerned. Once in a while she does something she can't believe she did. For instance, on one of her first nights in the dorm she ordered out for a pizza. "I took my wallet downstairs to pay the delivery person and then took my pizza back to my room. Three hours later I realized that I hadn't brought my wallet back to my room. I went downstairs, remembering that I had set my wallet on the table. By the time I went back, my wallet was gone," she says. Her driver's license, college ID and her credit cards were all in the wallet and would need to be replaced. "I still can't believe I did that," she says.

Above all, Ashley sees herself as an optimistic person. She smiles easily and likes to chuckle. She believes that she is a "smart cookie" who will do well her first semester of college. Her grades she predicts will be A in English Composition, A in First-Year Seminar, A in Pre-Calc, B in History and B in Critical Thinking. To get good grades in college, she plans on heeding the advice her mother gave to "stay focused and to have fun but not too much." Her father said to her, "You know what you're here to do." Ashley laughs about her father. She says, "He also told me not to give my number out to boys."

Reggie

"I'm not financially enrolled," is the first thing Reggie tells me after sitting down in my office chair and telling me he wants to participate in my project. "I can't find a co-signer for my loan," he says, with a quizzical look on his face, as if he doesn't quite believe what he's saying. So far he's been attending classes and living in the dorms while trying to find someone who will sign for him. If he doesn't find a co-signer soon he will be forced to go back to his home in Dallas, Texas. The logical person to co-sign for him is his mother but her credit was wrecked several years ago when she lost her job and was unemployed for a year, which caused financial difficulties. Reggie doesn't have much of a relationship with his father—he chooses only to see him about once a year. In total Reggie has asked five family members to co-sign for him but they have all turned him down. Even his own grandmother—his father's mother—said no. He says, "She's wanted to buy a new car and was afraid that co-signing a student loan for me would make it hard for her to do that."

Despite his constant worry that he's going to have to pack up and go home soon, Reggie forges ahead with the belief that he will remain a student here. He'd like to stay and be given the opportunity to redeem himself for his poor performance in high school, where he earned a 2.8 G.P.A. He says that in high school his "priorities were out of whack." He says, "I didn't have my future in mind." Instead of studying he spent his time on social media and hanging out with friends.

Reggie aims to be the first person in his family to complete college.

His mother is a high school graduate who works two jobs and he has a couple of cousins who dropped out of college. His mother has always encouraged her only child not to "make the same mistakes I made" and to pursue a college diploma.

A business major who would either like to go into marketing or education, Reggie says that no matter which he eventually chooses he wants to one day get his doctorate and possibly teach, though he's unsure at what level. While Reggie plans to study more than he did in high school, he isn't sure how much studying he'll need to do for the grades he aspires to achieve. His plan is to get A's in Biology, First-Year Seminar and Culture and Society, and B's in English, History and Algebra. So far what he has done to work towards those grades is set his phone to remind him when it is time to study.

Besides worrying about his financial situation, Reggie says two things that will be the biggest challenge for him are staying focused and remaining determined. He knows he needs to keep his mind on his priorities and not get carried away with the fun and freedom that college life offers. Coming to college, he had ideas that college would be like the TV show *A Different World*, where "everyone made good friends and always had something to do" and their problems always got solved. He knows, however, that that was just a TV show. In Reggie's world one minute he's on the phone listening to a family member say, "no, no, no" to co-signing his loan, and the next minute he's straightening his face and heading to his next class hoping that this won't be his last time.

Becoming a College Student

September 4

Tameka

Tameka tells me she spent the Labor Day holiday studying. She put in nine hours. Mostly she wanted to prepare for a quiz in her World Literature class. However, the instructor of that class forgot to give the quiz, "and I wasn't going to remind her," says Tameka. The only grade Tameka has received so far is a 100 for her homework in her Algebra class. At this point Algebra is her favorite class because she finds it easy. "The work covered in that class I learned back in the eighth grade," she says.

Currently, she's working on a three-page paper for her history class. It's due in a day and she has two pages of it completed. In her speech class she's trying hard to avoid giving her first speech. When the professor asks who wants to go next, "I hide behind the person in front of me," she says. Her shyness prevents her from volunteering to give her speech. "I'm going to avoid giving my speech for as long as I can," she says.

Some good news for Tameka in her search for a job at Walmart—she's had an interview and is waiting for the call back. She's confident she will get the job. She smiles when talking about it. Another thing that makes her smile is that she's joined the Biology club.

Tameka says that the best thing about college so far is that she wakes up every morning "knowing I can do anything I want to do." She says, "I call the shots here." The worst part is sharing a room, she says. Her roommate, she says, is "alright," but she doesn't like it that her roommate tells her to turn the volume of her TV down. As for the food in the cafeteria, Tameka describes it as "okay," but she's also quick to say that "I've been eating out a lot."

The worst thing that has happened to Tameka at this point is that one of her professors forgot to mark that she's been attending class and the Registrar dropped her from that class. "I had to spend some time at the Registrar getting re-registered for the class," she says. But the experience wasn't a total waste of time. The same thing had happened to a classmate in her history class and they spent time together at the Registrar's office. Since then they've been hanging out together around campus. Tameka has made a friend.

Michael

When I ask Michael about his roommate, he quickly and emphatically says, "I hate him. He called me 'over the top' and told me that he doesn't like me. I will never forget what he said to me." Furthermore, despite the fact that the outside temperature has been in the eighties and nineties, his roommate turns on the heat in their room. The thermostat is on his roommate's side of the room and Michael doesn't feel comfortable going over there and turning it down. Yet, Michael says that the dorms are "great" and that "the people are great. Everywhere I go I say 'hi' to all the people I know."

The food in the cafeteria he says is "okay." "Add salt and pepper and you'll be fine," he says. But then he says that the food in the caf also "makes you use the restroom."

Computer crashes have been Michael's main problem so far. One of his professor's computers crashed, causing Michael to be dropped from the class. And his own computer crashed, erasing everything he had on the hard drive. His computer problems were not the reason, however, that he didn't type his paper for his Culture and Society class. "I didn't know that all papers for college classes are supposed to be typed," he says. Still, he received a B plus on the paper.

His favorite class so far is English. "I love the diversity in opinion my classmates show in our class discussions," he says. He's also enjoyed the topics they've discussed so far: masculinity in men, Hip Hop, Jay Z and Harry Belafonte's criticism of him. Michael is looking forward to his upcoming speech in speech class. He says, "I've been working on it for two days and I can't wait to give it to the class." Improving his speaking abilities is something that Michael wants to work on since his career aspirations hinge on how well he can speak to groups of people.

Besides working on his speech, Michael has been busy joining clubs. "I've joined the Pre-Alumni Council, the SGA, the NAACP and the Campus Activities Board," he says. "And I auditioned for the fashion show at Homecoming. At first I was told that I didn't make it. When I went back to ask why, I was told that they had reconsidered and that I would be part of it."

When I ask him what he thinks of college so far, he says, "I love it."

Ashley

Ashley tells me that she's been doing a lot of reading for her history and Critical Thinking classes. She reads for about an hour and a half a day. Her favorite class is English because they have interesting discussions. "So far we've discussed an article that the governor of Louisiana Bobby Jindal wrote on race, and we've talked about music and pop culture," she says. "It was fun."

Thus far the worst thing that's happened to Ashley (besides having her wallet stolen) has been getting dropped from her classes. Like many students, she had to spend time at the Registrar getting that straightened out. "I didn't like having to do that," she says. Another thing she doesn't like so far is the messiness of the bathrooms in her dorm. "The girls throw their paper towels all over the place," she says. She likes her roommate though; they've known each other since the fourth grade and came to school together. She is a little worried however that her roommate might be a little peeved at her. "My roommate has eight o'clock classes every day and I like to stay up late watching TV shows on my laptop," she says. And then there was the night Ashley stood in the middle of the floor just "doing nothing" and her roommate woke up and kept saying, "What are you doing? What are you doing?"

Ashley says that cafeteria has "great pizza and great fries" but that "the chili looks like spaghetti. I'm a picky eater and so far I've been eating in the caf only the pizza, fries and salad," she says. "I miss my mom's cooking."

Ashley has made friends in the dorm. They like to sit in the common area and watch shows such as *Jerry Springer* and *Maury Povich.* She's also joined the Campus Activities Board and the Bold and Beautiful Society, which she describes as a group of "full-figured females who have group discussions about topics that have something to do with body types." Next she'll be trying out for the stroll team.

So far the best thing about college, Ashley says, is the freedom. "I control what I do with my time." The worst thing, she says, is that she can't go home. She misses her family. Fortunately for her a family friend lives in the area. Ashley spent the Labor Day holiday at this friend's house washing her clothes (the washers in her dorm are broken) and "sleeping in a comfortable bed." The bed in her dorm room is high, and she has to jump up to get into it or she has to use a step stool. Either way, she says, her bed is the most annoying aspect of her life on campus.

Reggie

Reggie pulled his first college all-nighter working on a paper for his Culture and Society class. "Then my professor didn't collect the paper," he says, sounding confused. In other classes he hasn't had any quizzes or tests so he is unable to gauge his performance so far.

While Reggie doesn't have a problem with the food in the caf or with his dorm, he doesn't particularly care for his roommate. They met through social media and Reggie thought he'd like sharing a room with him, but their personalities have clashed. "I'm more down to earth than he is," Reggie says. "I'm more realistic. My roommate is loud and likes attention and wants people to feel sorry for him," he says. They haven't spoken to each other in weeks.

Reggie has yet to join any clubs or organizations. He doesn't think he should since he still isn't financially enrolled. He looks dejected. He's having a hard time engaging in campus activities since he doesn't know how much longer he'll be a part of the campus. Worrying about his loan has become "a huge distraction." "I don't know if I should even be going to my classes," he says. We didn't talk for very long, since there didn't seem to be anything else to talk about.

New Roommate

September 11

Tameka

I wait in my office but Tameka doesn't show. I text her, asking her if she needs to reschedule. She texts back a half hour later, "I am sooooo sorry yes!!! I've been just so caught up . . . I started in Walmart." Great, I think. She got the job she wanted. I can't wait to hear about it. I also can't wait to find out if she gave her speech and how she did on her history test.

Michael

Michael is a no-show also, but when I text him, he says he forgot but is on his way. When he arrives, he tells me that he's cleaning his room every day even though it doesn't need it. "I move the furniture around, make the bed, sweep and mop the floor," he says. "You have your own mop?" I ask. "Sure," he says, "brought it from home." He's cleaning because the room is all his now. His roommate was moved out by the school for not paying his tuition. Michael has turned down the thermostat, making his room cooler. He hopes that he doesn't get another roommate and is able to live by himself. He says he's "heard a new roommate is coming." For the time being, though, he says, "I'm loving having the room to myself."

That's the good news. The bad news is that the car battery on his mother's new car needed to be replaced, costing his mother $105, which was the money she had promised to give to Michael so that he could buy the access code for his math class and do the homework on the website. When I ask him what he thinks about this turn of events, he shrugs. "Nothing I can do about it at this point," he says. He's also waiting for a refund check from the school for $600. "When I get it I'm going to use it to buy books for my classes," he says. "I've only been able to buy the book for my First-Year Seminar class. Everything would be so much better if I had my books," he says.

The speech he was looking forward to giving in his speech class turned out well. Michael smiles when I bring it up. The speech was a narrative of his life and he received 20 out of 25 points. The class gave him feedback. "They told me to slow down," he says. He got high marks from the professor for his eye contact and his diction, but was told not "to move around so much." "I have a habit of rocking," he tells me. "I need to stop that."

Other than the three hours he spent one day working on a blog for his English class, Michael hasn't been spending much time on class work. So far, he says, "There hasn't been much to study for." Instead he spends his out-of-class time hanging out with friends. They hang out in each other's rooms, eat lunch and late night dinner together, and they work out on the track. He also spends time talking to his friends over social media. "Sometimes I'm using my phone so much communicating with friends that it overheats and slows down," he says. When I ask him how he feels about all his friends, he says, "I love them!"

Ashley

Another no-show. What's going on? I wait, check my email. There's one from Ashley. It says, "Something came up with my family [.] I was wondering if I could [come] at another time." Uh oh, I think. If there's one thing I know about unforeseen problems that students encounter, it is that medical problems with family members often blindside them. I couldn't count the number of students I've had over the years who are distracted by them or who just disappear for long periods of time because of a medical issue that a family member is having. Grades usually suffer, and sometimes the student drops the class.

I email her back, asking when we can reschedule. For days I get no response. I text her. Nothing. Then, four days later she responds, saying that she'll meet with me at our usual time next week. I don't know what to expect. Now I'm worrying about what's going on with her. Her appointment to see me can't get here quickly enough.

Reggie

With Reggie's problem I expect him to be a no-show, and he is. I'm thinking that he's back in Texas. I text him. He responds and, amazingly, he says he can see me in two days. He's still on campus. Two days later when he arrives he says, "I had my bags packed and was already to head back home. I couldn't get a co-signer for my loan," he says. "They told me I had to move out." The manager came when he was at class and took his things, including his pet Beta fish, a gift the students in his school received when a classmate died. The fish was meant to be a living memorial to their dead classmate.

That day Reggie spoke to a financial aid employee who told him that the scholarship money he was awarded covered two classes and since he won't be paying for a dorm room or a meal plan, he could be financially enrolled for two classes. (He chose English and Biology.) He just needed to find somewhere to live.

His mother, who had been stressed out by what was happening to her only child, found family friends who live south of the school—a married couple with four children, one of them a special needs child—who agreed to let Reggie live with them. And since Reggie doesn't have a car, they told him that they would drive him to and from school. Happy to be financially enrolled, Reggie took them up on their offer and has spent the last couple days "trying to catch up on my classes."

This situation has forced him to alter his immediate goals. The first thing Reggie says he needs to do now is get a car. He can see that it will be too difficult for the couple he's living with to drive him back and forth to school for the entire semester. He doesn't have money for a car, so he has to get a job. "If I get a job, I can buy a car and be less of a burden on the family," he says. And, since he'd like to stick around for longer than one semester, his goal is to find grants and scholarships that will pay for his education.

Reggie tells me that "mentally I was in Texas and now I need to come back to school." He hadn't done any studying and hadn't written any papers. He says, "All my free time has been spent waiting on Student Accounts and trying to figure out what I was going to do." Now that he knows he'll be around for a while, he has given thought to changing his major and joining a fraternity at some point. Right now he says he just wants to hang on and see how this new situation turns out. He says, "It's times like these that you find out how strong you are."

Getting a Job

September 18

Tameka

Tameka is all smiles when she comes into my office. "I'm sorry about last week," she says. "I'm just so busy I forgot." She sits down and tells me about her job at Walmart. "Dealing with customers is hard," she says. "I'm a cashier five days a week. I told them I couldn't work past nine but they have me working till eleven every night," she says. She's putting between twenty-five and thirty-three hours in a week. She tells me her job is "something to get used to."

I ask about sleep. Is she getting any? "Not enough," she says. She goes to sleep around one in the morning and gets up at 6:50 because she has eight o'clock classes every day. "So you're getting around six hours a night?" I ask. "If that," she says. "I'm so tired."

Anxious to find out how her schoolwork is progressing, I ask about the history paper she was working on last time we spoke and also about the speech that she was trying to avoid. She says she got a 90 on the history paper, as well as an A on a Biology take home. She also got an A on her speech. "It was on a risk that you took that changed your life," she says. "I was crying. I spoke about a car accident that I caused with my sister in the car. I hit a ditch in the snow. My sister blacked out and I had to pull her out of the car. She didn't respond at first. Her leg was broken. That was an emotional class," she says. "I'm glad there weren't any guys in class that day. Only girls. I think after that speech it will be easier to give other ones."

As far as her other classes go, Tameka's biggest problem is her World Literature class. She is very frustrated with the instructor. "I can't get the code for Turn It In," she says. "I'm missing work. I ask her for it but she won't give it to me. I'm the only one without it. I keep emailing her." And the other day Tameka got back a paper she wrote for the class. She received a zero on it. "I spend more time on my World Lit. class than any other class," she says. "I got a zero on my paper because I wrote in pencil instead of pen. It doesn't say anywhere on the syllabus that you have to write in pen. I couldn't believe I got a zero." She says to me, obviously frustrated, "Tell the incoming freshmen not to write in pencil."

Moreover, according to the syllabus, a quiz would be given in the class on the 16th. Instead the instructor gave that quiz on the 14th, two days before the date scheduled on the syllabus. "I wasn't ready for the quiz on the 14th," Tameka says. I ask, "What did the instructor say about the date change?" Tameka says, "She said a mistake had been made. That's all she said." She pauses, says, "I still can't believe I got a zero on that paper. I just can't get through to her."

Because of her job, Tameka admits that she isn't putting in the amount of time she should for her classes. "I'm only putting in the minimum of time of work for my classes," she says. "I only get in about an hour to an hour and half each day. I am learning to focus on some classes more than others."

I ask about her social life. She laughs. "Ain't no social life," she says, "except socializing with customers." She says, "When I came here, I thought I could do it all—school, work, social life, my boyfriend. Now I'm learning, no, I can't." I ask about friends. "My suitemate and an upperclassman friend walk me home from work," she says. "My suitemate is considerate. The other night she made me a late-night dinner," she says. So far Tameka's boyfriend from home came to visit her once and stayed in a motel. She misses him and her family and wonders when, with her busy schedule, she'll get to see them again.

Michael

Michael sends me a text. "I won't be able to make it today. I'm taking a trip back home." I'll have to wait a week to find out how his trip home went.

Ashley

Fortunately, Ashley's family emergency wasn't as bad as I feared. Her mom went back to the hospital because of her foot. "I thought she was going to have surgery again," Ashley says. "I was on Oovoo with my family the whole weekend. I panicked," she says. "My family told me little stuff but not everything so that I wouldn't worry." Ashley spoke to her mom this morning and everything is okay. Her mother went back to work.

We quickly move on to talking about her study habits. She tells me she studies between her classes, MWF 12 to 1 and 2 to 4. Sometimes she studies in her room but when she's in her room she often takes a nap. Last night she says, "I was up till twelve working on a personal statement for English." It was due in the morning. "That was the only night I worked on it," she says.

She hasn't received any grades yet in her classes. On Friday she'll be getting back her paper in English. I ask her what she wrote her paper on. "Either Jay Z or Bobby Jindal," she says. "You can't remember?" I say. She shakes her head. "My mind is elsewhere," she says.

I ask about her roommate, if she's still bothering her roommate by watching shows on her laptop late at night. "She's starting to stay up with me," Ashley says, laughing. "What does your roommate say about living with you?" I ask. "She says it's an experience," she says. "I'm messier than her and less organized. She plans out what to wear the next day but I just try things on at the last minute until I find something I like."

Ashley has decided not to join the stroll team. She strained her knee so instead, "I stand on the side and cheer them on," she says. She's thinking instead she'll sign up for the step team.

"Anything interesting happen to you since the last time I saw you?" I ask. She thinks. "Oh, yeah," she says. "The doorknob on our door fell off, on both sides. Our door was unlocked for a week. The hall director told us to hide our valuables until it was fixed. They put a work order in. "We were on the emergency list and still it took a week for them to fix our door. My roommate and I set our iPods up to video the room in case somebody came in. But no one came."

As she's standing up to leave, I tell Ashley how good it was to see her, that I'd been worried. She gives me a look and a little laugh that says my worry was silly. I'm glad it was.

Reggie

Reggie lives in the room that had been an office. He has his own bathroom and isn't being charged anything to live in the house. But he says, "I will contribute eventually." It's a good set up. However, he's had to make some big adjustments. All together, there are six people in the family. Reggie says, "I'm not used to having all these people around. I'm used to just me and my mom. The first thing in the morning there's all these happy, talking people around me. Me and my mom aren't like that." And although everyone in the family goes to bed at nine, Reggie goes to bed later. "By ten I'm the only one still up," he says.

The family Reggie lives with moved from Texas eight years ago. Reggie's mother and the mother of the family were friends and pregnant at the same time, Reggie's mother with Reggie and the family's mother with her first born. He's their special needs child. When he was four he had a stroke he never recovered from. The other children are ages ten, fourteen and fifteen. The father is a pastor, who, Reggie says, "Shelters his kids. They have family movie night," he says, "but they're only religious movies. Those kids don't know how the world works the way I did at their age," Reggie says. And the children are homeschooled by the mother. "The other day she was teaching a lesson while I was eating breakfast. I looked at the title of the book. It said, *God and Science.* I looked at the other books, *God and Math*, *God and English.* I thought, what have I gotten myself into?" He laughs. "My life went from a reality show to a family sitcom."

He likes having his own bathroom and the meals they serve, that is when he's home in time to eat them. "They eat at four o'clock," he says. "When I don't get there till five, they've already eaten." The major problem for Reggie has been his commute to school. By car it is about a thirty-minute drive, but the other day no one could drive him so he had to take the bus to the train. "I was confused," he says. "I didn't know where to go." He desperately wants a car, and not just to use to go to school. The other day he needed a label from a sports drink for his Biology class. The mother said she would drive him to the store for one. "I told them just to stop off at the gas station and I'd go in and get one," he says. "But she didn't think it was a good idea to go to a gas station." Instead she insisted on driving further to get to Family Dollar. "I can't figure out why anyone would have a problem going to a gas station," he says.

Despite the strangeness of his situation, Reggie is in better spirits these days. You can see it in his face. He's glad to be a full-fledged college student now. "I'm happy to get my ID," he says. "Now I don't have to sneak on campus at night afraid that they'll throw me off when they find out I don't have an ID." Further, he spoke to his old roommate and they talked about their problems with each other. They didn't work everything out, but, Reggie says, "We left each other on a better note than when we started."

Now that he's an enrolled student, he's been studying every night from seven to nine thirty. His classes are now his priority, as opposed to worrying about getting a co-signer for his loan. Oddly enough, even though he doesn't have a loan, he's been informed that he will be receiving a refund check from the school for $700. "I don't know why I'm getting it," he says. "But I could use it to put towards a car."

Maybe Reggie's luck is changing.

First Grades

September 25

Tameka

"What would you like to tell me first?" I ask Tameka once we settle into our chairs and exchange pleasantries. "I got 67 on my Biology quiz and 64 on my World Lit. test," she says. "Only two people in the whole class passed the Biology quiz," she says. "The professor told us. He said everybody did terrible." I ask her why she didn't do so well. She says, "High school didn't prepare me for college. At least not my high school. I studied the book but the test was more conceptual. Our generation doesn't have to think. We just Google everything. I have to learn conceptual thinking."

As for her World Literature test, Tameka says, "I didn't know that we were supposed to read the prefaces to the works. A lot of that stuff was on the test. It wasn't covered in class." While she has gotten the code for Turn It In and her instructor has changed her grade for the paper she wrote in pencil, things are not going well for her in that class. "When I got my test back I was like, what—64? I couldn't believe it," she says. Later as we talked, Tameka asked me, "Is it too late to drop World Lit.?" My advice to her was to sit down with her instructor and tell the instructor that she is thinking of dropping and to ask what the instructor advises. She said that that was what she would do.

Last time we spoke Tameka had alluded to having a boyfriend at home. That was the first time she'd mentioned him so I bring up that topic. "We started seeing each other in January," she says. "He goes to trade school, heating and cooling," she says. I ask her how much time she has for a boyfriend, even one back home. "Not much," she says. "We talk on the phone every day and Oovoo sometimes." He has come to visit her twice.

Just as she told me last week, her schedule is hectic and she has little time for study and sleep. She's still working till eleven most nights and she's working hard. Walmart monitors how many groceries the cashiers ring up per hour. They want their cashiers to achieve between 900 and 1,500 scans per hour. Tameka is at 1,000, which makes her bosses happy. She is showing progress.

While Tameka's making her bosses happy, she's not making her roommate happy. Last week she told me that things were good between them but today she tells me a different story. "She's spoiled," Tameka says about her roommate. "She doesn't have to worry about anything. She doesn't have to work and her father pays all her bills. She doesn't have eight o'clock classes like me and she gets more sleep than me but she grumbles from bed when I come back from my job and complains about my alarm clock going off so early," Tameka says. "I got so many other things to deal with and now I have to deal with her too."

"I'm tired," she says. "It's a rough life."

Michael

Michael looks like he is about to bust when talking about his weekend trip back home. He's very excited and speaks rapidly. He says his trip home was "really intriguing." He had a long conversation with his three brothers down in their basement. They talked about many things but mostly about his time in college so far. "They saw my passion," Michael says. "They could tell how special my passion is." His twenty-three year old brother, who is also a freshman in college, told him that he is going to college for Michael as well as for himself. "My brothers told me they're counting on me," Michael says. "And I told them I'm counting on them."

Michael got to see his best friend, who was also home from college. "That was the best part of my day," he says. He was on the bus for four hours round trip and that is when he worked on an essay for his English class. He typed on his laptop. The bus trip cost him $22, but, while he was home, his parents gave him some money. One of his aunts also gave him money and two of his brothers did as well. He says he's using a portion of that money to buy the math access code that he'd been unable to purchase because of a lack of funds.

He's still waiting on his refund check from the school. "I'm going to use that money to buy a business suit," he says. "And front row Drake tickets and to stock up on food in my room." He says he's probably not going to use the money to buy books. "Not one of my professors is using books," he says. "Except for science. I might buy that one."

For three days now Michael has been living with a new roommate. "I told him I can't stand a dirty room," he says. "I like my room to smell good. I told him not to leave the bathroom a mess and to replace the used roll of toilet paper," he says. Other than that Michael says, "I don't talk to him. I really don't know him."

I ask about grades. "I got a B on my math test," he says. "That was pretty good. But I failed my Physical Science project. I'm a little lost in that class. I need a tutor," he says. Michael admits that he doesn't have a study schedule. "I just study whenever I need to. Sunday I will be doing all my work because Saturday I will be having fun," he says. "It's hard to manage partying and grades," he says. "But sometimes you gotta have fun."

"Anything unusual happened to you?" I ask. His smile broadens. "I helped these girls in the library make copies. I gave them my copy card and told them not to worry about it. They were from Gamma Phi Delta and they elected me Mr. Gamma Phi Delta." I ask him what he thinks about that. "I thought it was so cool," he says. "It's something I always thought I would want to do." When I ask him what his responsibilities are, he looks them up on his phone. He reads, "to uphold the office with dignity and respect, to host events with the queen and to participate in the homecoming parade."

I can tell by the blissful look on his face that he will take the responsibilities of the office seriously.

Ashley

Ashley enters my office wearing a chrome necklace with three inch letters that say "SWAG." I ask her about it. "I bought it from a person on the promenade," she says. "I bought it because it's cute."

Today, Ashley looks tired and rundown. I ask her about it. First, she says, because it's raining, then she says, "I'm trying to get a plane ticket to go home for this weekend. I miss my parents. I miss my bed and my mom's cooking. I want to go home and get an energy boost. Going home will make me feel better," she says.

Getting a 76 on her history test didn't help her mood any. "That's a test I really studied for," she says. "I studied with a study group for two hours the day before. I started studying for that test on Tuesday and I took it on Friday. I got to study harder for my next test," she says.

Ashley did join the step team as she said she would. They practice five days a week from 7 to 10:30 at night. "That's a lot," I say. "I have a hard time fitting in eating and studying," she says. "Sometimes I bring homework along and do it while they're practicing." She tells me that the show is at the end of October. I ask how long they will perform at the show. "Eleven minutes," she says. "Wow, all that for eleven minutes?" I say. "Do you ever ask yourself if it's worth it?" "All the time," she says.

I ask her if she's met any new people. "The second floor got a new microwave so I meet people there when I use the microwave. I make Oodles of Noodles in it," she says.

I'm having a difficult time talking to Ashley today. She looks a bit forlorn. Since her roommate has been a friend of hers for a long time, I think that asking about her will make Ashley feel better. I'm wrong. "My roommate makes me think of home," she says. "I want to go home."

Reggie

This time Reggie seems more distracted than usual. Whenever he's in my office he sets his iPhone on his lap and it flashes every couple of minutes as well as beeps, but this time, besides attending to his active phone, Reggie is pulling tape from my tape dispenser and playing with it. His eyes dart around. I start in about the family he's living with. "I went to church with them yesterday, Bible study. They sang." I ask why he went. "I want to participate more," he says. "I'll go again."

Further, the other day, he saw the eighteen year old have a seizure. "He fell down the stairs and cut his leg," Reggie says. "I was shocked but they acted like it was no big deal. They said he has them all the time. Last time, they said, he fell on the table and broke it."

Yesterday Reggie ate dinner with them. "We ate at 4:30," he says. "I was so hungry by ten. Of course, they were all asleep by then." Also, Reggie had what he calls "a very awkward" conversation with the mother. One night he told them he wouldn't be home. They called his mother and his mother called him and made it sound as if the family was making a big deal out of his not being home. The mother came into Reggie's bedroom the following day and said, "So." "It was very awkward," he says. "They're not up front people. They beat around the bush. She finally asked me what I was going to contribute. I didn't know what she meant. She said, 'So. What are you going to contribute.' I told her I didn't understand. Then she said that she didn't want to be in my business. It was awkward."

Reggie's first grade in college was a 68 on a Biology quiz. "I did better than what I thought I would," he says. "I'm still trying to make up what I missed." However, he adds, "If I get another low grade it will be devastating."

Reggie is becoming more involved with campus activities now that he's an official student. He went to a Homecoming meeting and a Greek meeting about hazing and he's helping a girl he met his first week at school campaign for Miss Freshman. "I put her picture on Instagram," he says, "and I hand out fliers."

I ask him what he thinks about college now that he's an enrolled student. "I like it now," he says. I can tell he's ready to leave—he's taken a couple of pieces of tape from my dispenser—so I let him go.

Studying for Tests and Writing Papers

Conventional wisdom holds that for each class students need to study for at least one to three hours a night. To put it another way, when I was in college, I heard that good students spent, between time in class and studying and writing papers, forty hours a week. What I took away from that number was that being a full-time college student should be treated like a full-time job. As a student, I learned quickly that when I treated college like a part-time job, I got part-time grades—mostly C's and D's. When I treated college like a full-time job, I got full-time grades, A's and B's.

Putting in time is just the beginning. What's doubly important is how students spend that time. How they spend that time will ultimately determine how well they will do. To begin, what should students do before they go to class? How should they prepare? Before students go to class they should have already read the material that will be covered in that class. Students should look at the syllabus and see what is to be covered and read that section of their textbook. I can think of no greater waste of time than when students sit in class not knowing what the professor is talking about because they haven't prepared themselves for the class. Those are the students who play with their phones or talk to classmates. They are the students who are easily distracted. Students who are prepared for the class are involved in class discussion, they ask questions.

Often what students fail to realize is that there is a direct correlation between preparing for class and being prepared for tests. Quite simply, when students prepare for class, they usually have a better understanding of the material long before they have to take the test. It becomes part of their knowledge base, making studying for a test all the easier. If students are learning the material for the first time when studying the day before the test, then that information is less likely to be retained. What successful students have learned is that it is always better to be an active learner, to go out and get the knowledge, versus being a passive learner. Passive learners sit back and hope that classroom lectures will fill them in with all the information they'll need. However, classroom lectures should only supplement what students already know, or are in the process of learning. Lectures should never be seen as the only source of knowledge.

When studying for tests, students should begin studying a minimum of four days before the test. Every night the text(s) and class notes should be read over multiple times. I found that for big tests such as finals what worked best for me was to write out the important things I needed to memorize, over and over again until I had these things memorized. Studying for a test only the night before is a recipe for disaster. It might have worked in high school, but it won't work in college where the material covered is usually more voluminous and complex. When students study nights in advance they have more time to absorb the material, thereby committing more of it to memory.

A note on distractions. I've had students tell me over the years that they study best when they are listening to music or when they have the TV on. Research, on the other hand, shows otherwise (Sullivan). Students are often proud of their multi-tasking abilities, but if good grades are truly their goal, then there is no reason to multi-task. Nothing should get between students and preparing for tests.

Just as students should begin studying for tests days in advance, so, too, should they begin writing their papers days in advance. Pulling an all -nighter to write a paper for a class might seem like what college students are supposed to do, but it is certainly the worst possible way to write a paper. The best papers are written by students who take time out of each day—at least four days before the paper is due—to work on writing it. The best advice I can give is to work on a paper one paragraph at a time over those four days. Students need to put aside a half hour or an hour a day to work on a portion of the paper. Papers written all at once will seem rushed and more than likely will lack development of ideas.

Furthermore, without a doubt, one of the best things students can do to prepare for tests and to write papers is to stop by their professors' office during their office hours. Professors are required to have and to post their office hours and to be in their office during those times. Those hours are for the students. Students must take advantage of them. They need to sit down with their professors one-on-one and have them help them prepare for tests and write papers. When writing papers, students need to write rough drafts and take them to their professors to ask for guidance. In my classes, the good students, the students who receive A's, often are the students who come by my office to seek my advice and guidance. They are active learners. They don't want to leave their grades—and their futures—to chance. Good students put in the time on their classes, they prepare for tests and papers, they seek out their professors and ask for guidance.

Complications

October 2

Tameka

Five minutes before our scheduled time, Tameka is already waiting at my door. I see her at the end of the hall as I approach. She doesn't see me and calls me; my phone is ringing. She has never been this anxious to talk to me before. I wonder what's up. She tells me right away as we're sitting down. She took my advice. "I spoke to my World Lit. instructor," she says. "It turns out that she was teaching from a different edition than the one we have. There was different information in her book. That's why I got the bad grade. She changed my D to a B. I'm staying in the class," she says. "I took a quiz today. It matched our book, and I think I did well." I ask her what she learned from this experience. "It's important to go to the professors' office hours," she says.

She has other things to tell me about her classes. "I need to find out if my Biology professor drops the lowest grade," she says. She had gotten a D on the first test. "There are only four exams in the whole class," she says. She had problems studying the material so she's taken to using flashcards and watching lectures of a different professor on Youtube. "I like the professor better on Youtube," she says. "He helps me understand the material better."

She gave another speech in speech class. "The professor told me my speech was in the B range," Tameka says. "She said I had my feet crossed and I was playing with my hair. I think I should have gotten an A," she says. "At least a low A. She dropped my grade for minor things. I stayed in the time frame, I knew what I was talking about and I dressed right." Her speech was on what it was like to live during the Jim Crow era. "I did a good job," she says. "I even cited my sources during my speech. I should have gotten an A."

In Algebra Tameka says that her classmates are complaining about their professor's not letting them use calculators on the test. "In high school they let you use them," she says. "But not here. That's a big difference from high school." Regardless, she's pretty sure she did fine on the latest test.

Things have been better at her job at Walmart. "I have a wonderful schedule this week," she says. "I only work till eleven on Friday. The other days I only work till eight." Because of this schedule she's getting more sleep, between seven and eight hours. "I feel better," she says. Her roommate though is still grumbling. "I said to her," says Tameka, "you picked me to be your roommate. I didn't pick you."

Since we are halfway through the semester I thought I'd ask some reflective questions. The first is about how her thoughts about college have changed. "I thought college would be like high school," she says. "It's not. I got knocked for a loop. Tests are much harder; the teachers don't provide study guides like in high school," she says. "And in college you need to be self-motivated."

I ask her what has surprised her so far. "My bad grades," she says. "My boyfriend told me that great high school students become average college students," she says. In other words, it takes more work to be a great college student than to be a great high school student. Also, Tameka says, "In college you got to learn how to think and work at making sure your brain retains the information." This is what she has learned about herself, that she needs to work on retaining information. "I don't retain information well and I learned that learning is different than memorizing the information. You also need to be able to apply it."

Another thing Tameka has learned is that she needs to read more, and not just "garbage," as she says. A classmate of hers told her to read James Baldwin's *Go Tell It on the Mountain.* "It was out in the library," she says, "so I'm reading a biography about him," she says. "I got to read more than ghetto stories. I've set a goal to read more." She says about her classes, "They should make you read more."

I told her that she might want to read the short story "Sonny's Blues" by James Baldwin, that it was one of the great stories in American literature. She wrote it down. She seemed as if she wanted to stay and talk more, but I'd run out of questions.

Michael

Michael is about fifteen minutes late. When he arrives he tells me he just came from taking a test in his science class. "That was really a tough one," he says, not with a discouraged look, though. He says it with his usual big smile, as if he were thrilled to take that test. He goes right into telling me that the latest speech he gave in speech class went "absolutely perfect." "My professor told me I had good diction and good articulation," he says. "My speech was on the drop out rate in America, how it causes adversity, low parent engagement, pregnancy and family issues." I ask him what grade he got, assuming that he's going to tell me he got an A. "One fifteen out of one fifty," he says. I ask him what that score means since it doesn't sound like an A. "I have no clue," he says. He pauses for a moment. He says, "I volunteered to go first. I thought she would take it easy on me if I was the first one. I guess volunteering to go first didn't help." Even saying this, Michael doesn't lose his smile and the usual excitement in his voice.

As for his other classes, he says they are "fine." Since I last saw him he says he attended the BET Hip Hop awards with his friends and that he's been working on coronation practice with the Gamma Phi Delta sorority. "I'm practicing walking with Miss Gamma Phi Delta," he says, "and trying to find an outfit for the coronation."

When it comes to how his thoughts have changed about college, Michael says, "My thoughts haven't changed. I felt the same way then as I do now. But I am beginning to feel more like a college student, especially since they lifted the curfew in the freshmen dorms," he says. "Now we can get pizza and all study together."

There's a long pause when I ask him what has surprised him. "There's not a lot of belligerent people," he says. "I thought there would be. I love this school." "Anything else?" I say. "My science class is harder than I thought it would be," he says.

I ask him what he's learned about himself. He says, "I'm the same all around. I have good days all the time." He looks up with his dreamy smile and says, "My friends say I look older, more like a college student. Also, I'm gaining a little weight." I use his last statement to ask him about the food in the cafeteria. He completely loses his smile. It vanishes totally from his face in an instant. "I don't eat that food," he says. "The only thing that's any good in that place is the soda and the juice," he says. "I make my own food; I have a microwave. I make sausage and bacon in it." I ask him if the food in the caf is a disappointment. "It's like not having air and heat in the dorms," he says. "I wish I had more of a choice."

Quickly, he changes the subject and the smile comes back to his face. "I talk to my friends who go to PWI's about this place," he says. "They always say, 'I wish I went to an HBCU.'"

I conclude by asking him what he hopes to achieve this semester. "I need to be on the Dean's List," he says. "I better pass my science class."

Ashley

Unfortunately Ashley didn't get to go home as she had hoped. Instead she and her roommate went to the house of the family friend who lives nearby. I ask if that visit did anything to cure her homesickness. "It helped," she says, "comfy bed." She is quick to add, "But it's not home." She also Oovooed her mom and dad to quell her homesickness. The boot is off her mother's foot and she is now able to drive. Ashley says that she doesn't think she'll be going home until Thanksgiving.

I ask about her grades. She got an 88 in Critical Thinking, which she is happy about, and a 78 in her math class. I ask her what she thinks of that grade. "It sucks," she says. She says, "I knew what I was doing, yet I didn't know what I was doing." Because of the low grade, she says she plans on going to the Math Lab.

"How have your thoughts changed about college?" I ask. She says, "I thought college would be a grand experience," she says, "but it's just like high school. Except here your teachers only care if you care, not like in high school where they have to care. And in college I thought my teachers would teach more. My math teacher," she says, "I don't get the way he teaches."

"What has surprised you?" I ask. She says, "The people in the dorms. I went to an all girls high school. I kind of had a feel for the way girls acted but here it's extreme. They're louder and they leave their hair all over the floor and sometimes they leave the bathroom dirty. They drain their noodles in the sink and don't take out the ones that fall in. They just leave them in the sink. And toothpaste too, it's all over the sink," she says.

"What have you learned about yourself?" I ask. "That I'm a very quiet person. I observe first, then I talk if necessary. And I thought I'd be doing better gradewise. I learned I need to read more, actually read, not just glance at it and summarize. In high school I just glanced at the books except for English class. My goal is to read more," she says.

Ashley doesn't have step team practice anymore. One of the girls quit and it was too late to get someone else. "It's sad," she says. "The whole hall is affected." I ask if it's freed up more study time for her. She shrugs. "I guess," she says. "I'm looking for something else to do in place of the step team," she says.

As I usually do, I ask how much sleep she's getting. "It's weird," she says. "I can't get comfortable in that bed. It's so small, and since it's so high, I'm afraid I'll roll off and fall on the floor. That floor is hard." She says on average she's getting fewer than six hours of sleep a night. "The days I feel tired are the days I have my eight o'clock classes," she says.

"Anything else you can think of that's happening?" I ask. "It's my dad's birthday," she says. I ask what she got him for a present. "Nothing," she says. "He always says he doesn't want anything, so I got him what he wants," she says. I laugh. We finish by agreeing that it's difficult to find something to give to parents.

Reggie

Reggie comes to my office early. "I'm going back home today," he says. "My braces are hurting me and I need them fixed. I'm taking a bus out of here and flying back on Monday," he says. I ask him if he's been homesick. "I'm not," he says. "But I'm glad I'm going home. My high school is having homecoming and I'm looking forward to seeing everybody and being back in my bed."

I ask him how long the bus ride to Dallas is. "It's seventeen hours," he says. "I stayed up all night so I'll be sleepy on the bus and use that time to catch up on my sleep. Also I'll work on my English paper on the bus," he says.

About his grades, he received a four out of a five on a Biology quiz and ten out of ten on an English assignment. Since he only has two classes, he says, "I have plenty of time to study."

I ask how his thoughts about college have changed. "It's not as bad as I thought it would be," he says. I ask him if that's because he's only taking two classes. At first he says no, then he says, "I don't know. Maybe. I got nothing else to worry about."

About how he's changed, he says, "I've matured a lot," he says. "Certain things don't bother me anymore." He says he's not worried anymore about being part of a group. "I'm not here to make friends. I'm here to get my degree."

What has surprised him? "That it's not like high school where everyone knows everyone," he says. "I used to be popular but here there are so many people. You can just be popular in groups. Now I'm just normal, like everybody else. I'm free to be who I want to be."

What have you learned about yourself? "If I really want something, I'll find a way to get it."

Reggie looks sleepy. His phone isn't on his lap flashing away as usual. He says, "I'm just ready to go home." I ask him if his mom misses him. "She's made an appointment for me at my orthodontist and is lining up fun things for us to do," he says. "She's taken off Thursday and Friday from work. She's pretty excited."

"Tell me all about your trip next week," I say.

Going Home

October 9

Tameka

Tameka says that since that first time she spoke to her World Literature instructor in her office and straightened out her problem, she has had many meetings with her. She says about meeting with her instructor, "She's gonna work for her money. I'm gonna make her."

In Biology she got 90 on a quiz and had a midterm this past Monday and is confident she did pretty well. For First-Year Seminar she's written two lyceums. On the one she got 93 and on the other 80. I ask her why she got an 80 on the second one. "I don't know," she says. She takes it out of her bag and hands it to me. Some words and sentences are underlined but there are no written comments that explain the grade. I tell her that she should meet with her professor to find out why she got only an 80. "I will," she says.

"On my First-Year Seminar quiz," she says, "I got 88. I didn't know who the Dean of Arts and Sciences is or the chair of the Biology department, or how many times you're supposed to meet with your advisor," she says. She shakes her head. "There are some pretty tough teachers here," she says.

The best thing that's happened to Tameka this week has been her schedule at Walmart. "I'm only working till six or five thirty," she says.

"I'm off Friday and Saturday." I say that maybe someone is taking it easy on her now. "The computer," she says. "It's a computer-based schedule."

I ask her what she does with the money she's making. "Most of it goes into my savings account," she says. "What doesn't go in there is spent on food." "But you have a meal plan," I say. "The caf food is nasty," she says. "The meal plan isn't worth it."

Since Tameka brought up wanting to read more, and aware of the link between reading and success in school, I ask Tameka more about her background with books. I ask how many are in her home. "About a hundred," she says. "Children's books, dictionaries, textbooks never returned to school and 'hood stories," she says.

She tells me her mother "hates reading," that her brother doesn't read and that her sister reads a little. As for her, when she was little she read "Magic Tree House books, Junie B. Jones, teenage books and motivational books." She says that on her own she reads about thirty books a year. "Anything that interests me," she says. "Not Biology books." I ask her if she thinks reading makes you a better student. "It depends on what you read," she says.

Before we finish, I ask her how it's going with her roommate. "I'm not talking to her," she says. "I don't care about her. She still bugs me about turning my TV down. I talked to my mother about it and she told me I don't need to turn my TV down for her. She can complain all she wants."

Michael

Michael comes to my office wearing black-framed glasses. Since I've never seen him wear glasses before, I ask him about them. "Part of my fashion sense," he says. "So you don't need them?" I ask. "No," he says, pushing them up on top of his head.

Just like last week, Michael is quite late to my office. And just like last week, he says he just came from taking a science test. I ask him how it was. "Stressful," he says. The other day he says he visited his science teacher's office and spent two and a half hours studying for this test. On the test he took last week he got a 49. "Is that what I think it is?" I ask. "An F," he says. "But I got to do a forty point extra credit assignment which made my grade 89," he says. "I'm no longer failing," he says with his usual wide smile.

"My English class," he says, "is starting to get tough. She takes off for every little thing," he says. "She's eating us alive. I got 52 out of 100 on my outline." I ask what grade that number equates to. "I have no idea," he says. "In college they don't tell you too much about your grades," he says.

Next Michael tells me that he recently had a conversation with a friend from high school in which they discussed the differences between high school and college. "She said she missed sneaking out to eat lunch and skipping classes," he says. "I miss skipping classes too," he says. "Here it's no big deal if you do. No one says anything. It's your grade. And you pay whether you go to class or not." "You haven't skipped any classes?" I ask. "Sometimes in Society and Culture," he says. "I sign the roll and leave after ten minutes if I know we're not doing anything. Lots of students walk out. There're seventy students in that class so you don't standout if you do."

Michael says he's happy today because one of his brothers is in town and brought Michael a package containing the shirt he's going to wear to coronation. I ask how the coronation practice is going. "It's so irritating," he says. "I can't dance and we're dancing at it. The dance instructor doesn't have it together and there're so many people. And the professor who's over the whole thing talks to us like we're children. It's too much," he says.

The big event for Michael in the past week has been his taking a break from his group of ten friends he hangs out with. "I just needed a break from them," he says. "I stayed in my room Monday, Tuesday, Wednesday and ate by myself. I was just spending too much time with them. They asked where I'd been and I told them I just needed a break from you all. I feel so much better now."

I ask about books in his house. He looks up into the air as if considering. "There are about three hundred fifty to four hundred books in our home," he says. "My mom is a big reader. She reads African American adult fiction. There are a lot of cookbooks since my dad is a cook. And computer books for my dad because he's computer illiterate. My brothers read adult fiction books, but I don't like to read." At first Michael tells me he doesn't read on his own, but then he says he has read books that have meant something to him—*The Skin I'm In* by Sharon Draper and *Letters to a Young Brother* by Hill Harper. I ask if he thinks reading is important for college students.

"Yeah, reading is fundamental," he says, smiling.

Ashley

When Ashley arrives, she says she just got back from the mailroom. Her parents sent her a package. They sent two of her sweaters, some Utz potato chips (because she can't find them in the stores here) and S'mores pop tarts.

She tells me that after getting her package she went to the caf. "What did you get?" I ask. "Pizza," she says. "How was it?" "Nasty," she says. "That pizza is nasty. It just wasn't good."

She also tells me that for the first time she has gone to one of her professor's office hours to talk to him. "I talked to my First-Year Seminar professor," she says. "He overturned a zero he had given me.

He made a mistake and fixed it."

Intrigued that Ashley and her roommate have been friends since the fourth grade, I ask her how it's going. I have had students tell me that when they shared a dorm room with their friends, they ended up hating them by the end of the school year. Ashley says, "Yesterday we were up till two in the morning. We were just talking. I couldn't get comfortable. I couldn't sleep—that bed." I ask if their friendship has changed at all. At first she says that their friendship is tighter, that they do most things together, such as go to lunch and dinner, but then she says, "We argue more than we used to. Before we used to argue once in a while how I never stop talking. Now we argue every day over how I never stop talking."

I ask about books. She says that there are about one hundred books in her home. "We have a bookcase full of books," she says. "My mom reads mysteries and Dad reads motivational books." Ashley says she reads "only if it's a really good book, a mystery." I ask her in the past year how many books she's read on he own. "Maybe one," she says. "Do you think reading makes you a better student?" She says, "It's probably better than doing nothing. It extends your knowledge, increases your vocabulary, helps with critical thinking. But there are other outlets for those things. I watch the news instead, read stuff on the computer about current events, celebrity gossip," she says.

As she's leaving, Ashley tells me about her time in college so far: "Everything is starting to level out. The routines are all there." And she tells me she's going home in two weeks. Another family friend in the area will be driving her and her roommate back to Maryland.

Reggie

Reggie comes into my office, plugs his phone charger into my outlet, sits down and tells me about his trip. "I spent three hours in the bus station," he says, "because the bus was late. It was creepy with all the weird people staring at me the whole time. I didn't like it. The bus finally came. Our seventeen hour trip turned out to be a twenty hour trip," he says. "There was this big woman with two kids speaking Spanish on the phone the whole time. She was loud. In the middle of the night when we were all trying to sleep, she yelled out for the bus driver to stop the bus. She said the man across the aisle, who was sitting next to her nine or ten year old son, was trying to touch him. The man said he wasn't trying to touch her son. She got real loud and was trying to fight the man. She was throwing punches at him. This was at three o'clock in the morning on the freeway in Mississippi. The bus driver stopped the bus and we had to wait for the cops to come. I was thinking, this is not happening to me.

"An hour passed by, the police came and asked questions, the man didn't get on the bus and we took off," he says. Reggie thought that that was the end of the delay on his trip home. "We kept making all these stops," he says. "All over the place—Mississippi, Louisiana, so many in Texas. We even stopped at a bus station twenty minutes from my stop. People just kept getting on and off." I ask him if he wrote his English paper as he had planned. "No," he says. "I wrote it Monday on the plane on my phone. I sent it to a friend who turned it into a word document."

Back home Reggie got his braces fixed, ate at Water Burger, his favorite burger place, went to his high school and talked to his old teachers, went to a college football game with friends, then to a "kickback" at a friend's house, among other things. I ask him if he had the conversation with his mother about what he's going to do next semester. "No," he says, "we didn't." "Do you know what she wants you to do?" I ask. "She wants me to go to the University of North Texas, but I want to stay here and find scholarship money." Overall,

Reggie says about his trip home, "It was like I never left, like I dreamed about being in college."

If his trip back home wasn't eventful enough; his trip back to school and back to the family he lives with proved to be more than Reggie wanted to deal with. His plan was to fly into the airport Monday and take the train straight to school so he could go to class and turn his English paper in. The problem was he needed someone to pick up his suitcase, which he says weighed about fifty pounds, and take it back to the house. He called the mother of the family he lives with and she agreed to pick up his suitcase. But then at the airport his mother called him to tell him that the mother called her and said that she decided that she wasn't going to pick it up and that Reggie was a big boy and that he should figure it out on his own what to do. " 'What the hell,' I said. This is no time to be teaching me life lessons." He ended up leaving his suitcase at unclaimed baggage and was told that he had to pick it up by five or it wouldn't be there when he returned, which increased the amount of stress he felt. He had to get on the train and come to school, turn in his English paper and go to Biology class then rush back to the airport. "I just made it," he says. "I got my bag."

"When I got back to the house I didn't want to talk to her," he says. But she talked to him. "She told me how people are always trying to take advantage of her. That when other people learned that she was homeschooling her kids they just dropped their kids off so she could homeschool them. Then she says to me, 'I don't see a lot of humility out of your generation.'" Reggie said, "What are you saying to me?" "She said to me, 'You should be more of an asset to this house. You don't do any bad but you don't do any good.' She said to me that she didn't miss me when I was gone but she should have. Then one of the kids said, 'Maybe Reggie doesn't like us. He doesn't talk to us.' That's when I told them I didn't like living there and having to rely on them." Reggie laid it on the line. They argued and argued until the oldest boy had a seizure and that stopped the argument. Reggie says he was so exhausted by the day that he fell asleep on the floor.

After telling me all that it felt out of place to ask him about reading books, but I went ahead with it anyway. He says there are about one hundred books in his house and that his mother reads romance novels. When I ask him how many books he reads a year, he says, "Maybe two." He likes Sharon Draper's books *Foraged by Fire* and *Tears of a Tiger* because he finds them "relatable." When I ask him if he thinks reading makes you a better student, he says, "I guess."

Why Reading Matters

When I was in school I thought reading was just something that smart kids did. If you were born smart, I reasoned, you read books, just like if you were born an athlete, you hit home runs or threw a football fifty yards. I figured if you were born to do those things, you just naturally did them. What I would learn later was that smart kids were smart because they read, and that the more a person reads, the smarter that person becomes. I learned this the hard way. I was a lousy student in school, mediocre at best. I just got by. I didn't read books, or much of anything. I was such a poor student that my high school didn't bother ranking me. Eventually, I got it in my head that I needed to go to college. I entered college as a non-reader. I did poorly. Then I discovered books and I couldn't stop reading. Once I became a reader, I made the Dean's list. Repeatedly. I became one of the smart kids.

Over and over studies show that the number one factor that determines how well students will do in school is how well they read. By the fourth grade, students who aren't proficient in reading are four times more likely to drop out of high school (DellAntonia). According to the economists Steven Levitt and Stephen Dubner, if you want to know how well a child will do in school all you need to do is count the number of books in that child's home (174-75). Few books usually mean the child will do poorly. Many books mean the child is more likely to succeed in school. A home with books usually means the parents read, and when the parents read, the children often will model their parents' behavior and become readers themselves. Just about every educator—from preschool to college—will tell you the same thing—students who read and read often do better in school than those who don't.

What about college students? If students have made it to college that means they're smart enough, that they don't need to read books, right? That belief is held by many students. They have their phones, their laptops, their DVRs and so many other things that have taken the place of reading, so why read? The first and simplest answer is grades. Whenever I have a student who struggles reading aloud in class or who turns in papers that are written in butchered English, I inevitably ask the student one simple question—How much do you read on your own? The answer is always a variation of "I only read what's on my phone. Other than that, I don't read." Those students who don't read often don't pass basic classes such as English Composition, let alone achieve any kind of respectable G.P.A.

On the other hand, when I have students who do stellar work, who write effective, thoughtful essays, I ask a different question. I ask, "What books have you read lately?" Those students who do high quality work will rattle off a list of books they've read in the past weeks or months. Are these students atypical of people who succeed? Are they different from people who have done great things? No. Just about every great thinker, inventor, writer, leader—you name it—is, or was, a reader. Bill Gates recently said in an interview that wherever he travels he takes a suitcase full of books to read. Moreover, presidents and people who hold high offices are usually voracious readers. It's safe to say that if Martin Luther King, Jr. hadn't been a reader he wouldn't have been nearly as effective a writer, speaker or leader. And is there a better example of how important reading is than that of Malcolm X? While in prison, he read fifteen hours a day, and that reading completely changed the course of his life. He says, "As I see it today, the ability to read awoke inside of me some long dormant craving to be mentally alive" (179). The list of important and successful people who read is endless.

What does reading do for the reader? So many things. Here are the highlights. Reading improves a person's vocabulary, which improves language ability, which makes it possible for the reader to learn new concepts and ideas. Reading improves a person's concentration and focus. Reading teaches readers about the world around them, helping them to understand other beliefs, customs and thoughts. Reading improves imagination and memory. Reading teaches empathy. There's nothing like reading a book by or about someone different from yourself to change your perception of that person or about that type of person. Possibly, most importantly, reading improves a person's analytical and critical thinking skills. Employers in nearly every field say that they want employees with critical thinking skills. Employees who can think through problems and analyze ideas and concepts are highly prized and sought after and are well paid. Finally, reading improves your writing ability. Because reading does all the things listed above, it is the key factor in improving one's writing ability. Ask any college student if he or she doesn't see a need to write well. Writing well is essential to being a good college student.

What should college students read? Of course, books for classes should be on the top of the list. They should be read and reread. Beyond that I would suggest reading books that have something to do with the students' majors. Professors would be the best people to ask to get a list of books and writers in their fields. Further, I would suggest students read books about topics they are interested in. Any topic that students have a curiosity about would make a perfect place to start. Also, students should read fiction and nonfiction. Both types will enhance the students' thinking ability. I suggest that any time students read a writer whose work they enjoy or got something out of, students should seek out other titles by that writer and give them a read. When in doubt about what to read, students can also browse the first floor of the library and see what books are on display. Chances are they will find something that captures their interest. The point is that students need to make reading part of their daily life. When they do, they will become better students—and that's the bottom line.

Midterms

October 17

Tameka

Tameka texts me that she can't make it. Her schedule at Walmart has changed and she will be working at the time we usually meet.

Michael

Michael is a no show. I text him and ask him if we should reschedule for next week. He texts back, "yes."

Ashley

Ashley reports that she got a 90 on her history midterm test and a 100 on her math midterm test. When I ask her about her other classes, she shrugs. "Any papers in English?" "I don't know," she says. "I think we did something with grammar, with commas. Oh, yeah, I got 80 on a grammar diagnostic test."

She says that she's been studying more this past week, getting ready for her midterms. She's been studying three to four hours a day. She studies by herself in her room with her headphones on. She puts what she's studying to the song she's listening to, so if she's studying terms, she works those terms into the song. "It works for me," she says.

At the beginning of the semester Ashley said that she worried that going to parties might interfere with her schoolwork. I ask her about that. "It's not interfering," she says. "I only go to parties on the weekends and not weekdays. Weekdays are for school. Saturday is my me day," she says. "I stay away from schoolwork that day. I just relax and do what I want."

This weekend though she won't be partying. She'll be going home.

I ask her what her biggest conflict is in her day. Her answer is sleep. "When I come back from my classes I just need to sleep," she says. She gets so tired by mid-afternoon. I ask if she's tired because she has a hard time sleeping on her bed at night. "That's not as much of a problem," she says. "I'm getting used to it."

Best thing in your day? "After classes are over. Then I can relax, can wind down. On Tuesdays and Thursdays I'm not done with my classes till 4:30."

What is the most fun thing in your day? She makes a quizzical look. "It's hard," she says. "Not sure. I can't come up with anything."

Something you dread in your day? "My eight o'clock class," she says. "I have a hard time getting myself up before normal hours. Next semester I am going to try to avoid eight o'clock classes."

What are you looking forward to in your collegiate future? "I'm looking forward to getting into the education program, getting these basic classes behind me. I can't wait to focus more on what I'm getting my degree in—that, and graduating."

I ask her about her roommate. "We had our first real argument," she says, "no laughing and both of us put on our headphones for about an hour and a half. It got quiet." I ask what the fight was about. "I can't remember," she says. "What was it? I don't know." I ask if they made up. "We started talking about something else," she says. "That's how we made up."

She says that living with her friend from home has caused her to vocalize her opinions more. "I'm a very indecisive person," she says. "But with my roommate I'm becoming more vocal than I used to be and giving my opinion."

Another way in which she's changed is that she's less nervous around large numbers of people. There are fifty students in her history class and the class is focused on discussions that each student is expected to partake in. "At first I was nervous having all those eyes staring at me," she says. "But that's getting better." She's losing some of her nervousness.

I finish by asking her if anything has made her smile today. "Yes, the food in the caf was actually good today," she says. "The chicken and rice made me smile."

Reggie

Reggie says that he didn't finish his talk with the mother about why she didn't pick up his bag at the airport. But she has been talking to him. "She told me I didn't need to eat dinner with them anymore," he says. "I knew why she was saying that. There's a lot going on at that dinner table that I'm not used to," he says. "The ten year old is really hyper and constantly talking all the time; both the dad and the ten year old are narcoleptic and the youngest girl has a problem with her limbs where they just give out, they just stop working. And the fifteen year old stutters and takes a long time to get out what he wants to say. He's so excited to talk about his day and he keeps on stuttering away." Reggie says that while all that is going on the oldest child, the eighteen year old with seizures, insists on serving everybody food. "I don't like that," Reggie says. "I prefer to spoon out my own food. I don't need him to.

When he does, he makes a mess. And when he eats he smacks his lips together real loud."

If that isn't enough, the mother asks them questions while they're eating that they're supposed to answer, including Reggie. He says, "The other day she asked, 'Do you think what you do with your life matters?' I told her what I knew she wanted to hear. I said, 'No, it doesn't matter. It's what God wants.' She knew from the way I said it that I didn't believe it. That's why she told me I didn't need to eat with them. But I said I would eat with them, just don't make such a big deal about it."

Away from the dinner table the mother asked him what he's going to do about next semester. He told her he's looking into scholarships and has filled out some forms. "The whole house thing," she said to him, "so when will you be leaving us? Early December or late December? It should be early December," she said. "I just don't want you leaving here saying that we didn't help you." "By that point I was mad," Reggie says. "The whole thing just rubbed me the wrong way. She's got problems. I'm walking on eggshells around her. I never know how she'll react to me. She's got all those kids but she told me that she didn't want kids and she didn't want to work. Her husband wanted a big family so they struck a deal where she didn't have to work and they'd have a lot of kids. She's taking all her problems out on me," he says. "She won't even give me their Netflix password. When I asked for it she said, 'Let me come down and put it in for you.' And the other night they went to MacDonald's and didn't get me anything. She's something else." I ask him what his mother says about all this. "She just thinks it's funny," he says.

At first the father drove Reggie to school and picked him up. Now they drive him the ten minutes to the airport where he gets on the train to school. That isn't going smoothly. The other day when he tapped his card to get through the gate the message read that his card was already in use. He had money on his card and it should have worked fine. He told an employee, but, as Reggie says, "She had an attitude." She told him his card was out of money, but he told her it wasn't. He tried the card again and got the same message. He told the woman but she told him it was his fault and not the card's. So he tried the card again and got the same message. He told the woman and she came over to see. When the message appeared she let him through with her card without saying a word to him. "She looked dumb but didn't want to admit it," Reggie says. "I missed two trains!" he says.

As for his grades, he reports getting 86 on his Biology midterm and he has no idea about his grade in English.

I ask him what his biggest daily conflict is. "Dealing with the mother," he says. "What about at school?" "I love coming to school," he says. "Every day I wake up just waiting to go to school." If he does have a conflict at school, he says, it's his English professor. "She's kind of mean," he says. "She has a side to her."

The best thing about school, he says, is "seeing my friends and going to classes." Today he is going to a meeting of the Texas club, he says. "I'm trying to get more involved."

I ask him what he looks forward to in his collegiate future. He says, "A day when I'm a full-time student, when everything is exactly how I want it to be." "How do you deal with your situation now?" I ask. "I just go outside and walk around," he says. "I get out of that house and just walk."

Homecoming

October 23

Tameka

Tameka gets a different work schedule every week. This week's is different from last week's, so she is able to meet with me. She tells me what her mid-term grades were: World Literature B, Biology B, First-Year Seminar A, History B, Algebra B, Speech A. I ask her what she thinks about her grades. She says, "I think they're good, especially since I'm working. But I'm not going to rest on my laurels. I know my B's could be A's." She's not happy that she got 79 on her World Literature midterm test, but, she says, her instructor is working with her because she sees Tameka is trying. While Tameka says that she finds her World Literature class to be "halfway decent," it remains her biggest worry. "World Lit. stresses me out," she says. She's worried about their current project in the class. They're to take the lyrics of their home state's anthem and make a state poster which incorporates the anthem in the poster. This project will count as a regular test. "That's easy if it's Georgia," she says. "They have the Ray Charles song 'Georgia on My Mind.' Virginia's song is about how great slavery times were." Then she says, "Here I am, making a poster for my World Lit. class. I'm not an artist. I'm a Biology major!"

Tameka went to her First-Year Seminar's professor's office to ask about the 80 she got on her second paper. More important than the grade, she wanted to know why there were no comments on the paper explaining the grade. "He told me he grades the second paper harder," she says. "But he didn't say how. I don't know what he took points off for. He didn't say why he didn't write any comments, just that the second paper is graded harder."

I ask how things are going with her roommate. "She's okay. We don't talk," she says. "She wanted to have a talk with me. So we did. She told me that I did things out of spite like with my TV. I told her I'm trying to be respectful. I showed her how loud my TV could get and then I turned it down to the volume that I usually have it at. When I had it up loud, I said, 'This is what spiteful sounds like!' Then I turned it down. The only things we say to each other now is hi and bye," she says.

The first time we spoke Tameka told me that she was afraid that her shyness would hold her back. I ask her if it still does. "Probably," she says. "But I speak more." Seeking out a job was something she wouldn't have done in the past. "I went in there," she says, "and sought out the manager. I talked my way into a job." Another way she's speaking up more is by going to her professors' offices when she needs to. She isn't shy about doing that anymore.

Biggest conflict in your day? "Not getting enough sleep. I wish I could take naps in between school and work."

Most fun thing in your day? "Interacting with the people who live on my hall. And talking on the phone to people at home."

What do you dread most in your day? "Oh my God!—homework, studying. My mind goes elsewhere when it's boring. In Biology we were studying photosynthesis. I found myself looking at my laptop, my TV, my phone. Sometimes what we study is so boring."

What do you look forward to in your collegiate future? "Dropping Walmart and being an intern at a dentist office."

Michael

It's a chilly day and Michael comes to my office with a scarf wrapped around his head, from under his chin to the top of his head, almost as if he has a hood on. He sits there with it on the whole time we talk. I ask him about his mid-term grades. He tells me, B in Science, C in Speech, D in First-Year Seminar, D in Algebra 2 and B in Culture and Society. He didn't mention his grade in English.

I ask him about the D in First-Year Seminar. "I don't know how I got that," he says. "I want to see the test and see what I got wrong. I felt confident and thought I did well. I really need to step up my game." For Algebra, he says, "I gotta be more careful on tests, too many careless mistakes. About his speech class, he says, "I actually need to get the book and read it."

Overall, he says about his performance so far: "I'm not studying enough. I need to have a study skills session. Maybe some tutoring. I really don't know how to study. I need help." Even though his science mid-term grade was a B, Michael says he's close to dropping the class. "On the last test I got 26 out of 100," he says. "I have to go to his office hours. I don't understand."

Away from the classroom, Michael has been busy. He went to the fashion show but didn't participate because "I didn't make the cut." He went to coronation and describes the event as "great." He says, "It made me feel grand and rich. I love to see people dressed up in tuxes and dresses."

He also went home last weekend and met up with thirteen of his friends. "The weekend was all about my friends," he says. "We spent so much time together, clubbing, dinner and parlaying. I had a really good time," he says with his big, dreamy smile.

I ask about his new roommate. "He's nasty," he says. "The same trash was sitting in the room that was there when I left for home. The whole time I was home he didn't take it out. I asked him if he was going to take it out. He says he would, tomorrow. I told him now. He said he was a clean person, but he's not. That's it with him. I don't even know his name. I don't talk to him."

Biggest conflict in your day? "Getting up at seven thirty for my nine o'clock class. I would like classes that start at eleven."

Best thing in your life at this moment? "Being free. So much freedom. It's cool to know you can do what you want to do."

Most fun thing in your day? "My naps are so fun. Naps are everything. On Monday, Wednesday, Friday I nap from twelve to about one fifty and on Tuesdays and Thursdays from one to four. I might get another nap later in the day." I ask him when he fits in his studying. "From midnight to two," he says.

What do you dread the most in your day? "Going to speech class, my professor. I don't learn anything in that class. And it's a late class, four thirty to five forty-five. It's dreadful. It interrupts my naptime." "You had high hopes for your speech class," I say. "I know. Next speech class I'm going to take another professor."

What do you look forward to in your collegiate future? "Interning with any radio or TV station and in six years working for Enews and hosting red carpet events."

I go back to his study habits. "If you had to give up your naps or your friends in order to find time to study more, which would you choose?" "I would give up my friends to study more," he says. "I allow them to get in the way of studying. But on a normal day, I don't know what to study. I'm a little lost right now."

Ashley

The drive home to Maryland took ten hours. Ashley went home with her roommate and a friend of the family who drove her stick-shift car. Since Ashley doesn't know how to drive stick shift, she didn't drive and spent most of the time in the car sleeping. The first thing she did when she got home was to have her hair done. It's now braided. After that, she spent time with her family. "We had so much fun and we didn't even do anything," she says. She says the best part about going home was sleeping in her bed. "I got a great night of sleep," she says. "I felt great."

Sunday they had a big dinner with family and friends. She says that she realized that she missed her father more than anyone else. "I talk to my mom all the time, but not my dad," she says. "He says that he doesn't want to bother me." I ask her if she didn't want to go back to school, if on Sunday night she wanted to stay at home. "No," she says. "I thought to myself, now I'm ready to go back to school. I'll be fine for another six weeks." I ask her if she sees that as a sign of growth. She nods. "Yes," she says. "I told my parents I like school." She also wanted to go back to school because she missed her roommate. "I wasn't used to being without her for twenty-four hours."

For her mid-term grades, Ashley got A's in First-Year Seminar, Pre-Professional Seminar and Critical Thinking. She got B's in English and history. About these grades, she says, "I'm happy for the most part."

I ask her how studying is going. "It's been delayed a little bit lately," she says. "I've been skimping in what I do because of going home, going to a concert and going to Homecoming stuff." She says that "After Homecoming everything will be back to normal."

Reggie

Reggie's mid-term grade for both of his classes, English and Biology was a C. He explains that because he had not been financially enrolled his classes were dropped for a while and in that time he missed a quiz in

Biology and a paper in English. "I'll be able to make those up," he says. "My final grades will be higher."

As always I ask about his life with the family since that aspect of his current situation overwhelms him and occupies his mind more than his two classes. He tells me he and the mother had a heart-to-heart talk. "I told her how I feel and that she needs to be more direct when talking to me." He also told her about things that she said to him that he didn't like. For example, one night when they went to Popeye's, Reggie signed the slip after paying and accidentally took the pen. "She told me that that's a sign that I don't care about other people's property," he says. He told her she has to stop saying things like that. Since the talk, Reggie says it's been easier living with them, that "We talk more to avoid miscommunication. She got to know me more," he says.

One of the things they talked about was the fact that her eighteen year old with the seizures will always be someone she has to take care of because he suffered brain damage when he was five and will always have the mind of a five year old. "I said to her that it must be hard for her because she was pregnant with him when my mom was pregnant with me and here I am normal and in college," Reggie says. "You think she's jealous?" I ask. "Yes," he says.

I ask Reggie if he has any conflicts with the father. "No," he says, "he's fine. He told me first thing, as long as I don't touch his CDs and his DVDs and keep my feet off the couch, everything will be fine."

Reggie continues to eat dinner with the family in order to fit in and not cause problems, and he went with them to church Sunday to hear the father deliver a sermon. The father is a chaplain for a company and also a pastor at a church, whose congregation, on this Sunday, consisted of eleven people, seven of whom were the family and Reggie. They were all dressed up, the males in suits, but Reggie says he was purposely underdressed. "I wouldn't put on a suit for that," he says.

On his phone Reggie has a bible app that he used at the service, but one of the women parishioners saw him using his phone and told him to give it to her. "I didn't know her," he says. "I told her, 'You're not taking my phone!" He showed her his bible app and she backed off.

"Only eleven people?" I ask. "Is it a full service?" "Oh, yeah," Reggie says. "He be really preaching too! It's like an hour and a half long. The kids set up the projector that shows the bible scripture. They pray for like fifteen minutes, sing three hymns, then go around to each person saying what happened during the week. When they got to me, I said, 'I'm good,' and I didn't say anything. The whole time I'm there I'm thinking we could have done all of this at the house." I ask if he listened to the sermon. "I went to the bathroom," he says. "I spent time looking in the mirror, playing with my hair."

At the end of the service the woman who tried to take his phone apologized to Reggie. Reggie says, "If she tries to sit near me next time, I'll move."

Now that he's had a talk with the mother, Reggie says it's not her who bothers him. It is instead the hyper ten year old. "That boy is starting to irritate me. He likes to watch me get ready for school." He said to Reggie one day, "You look like a totally different person after you get ready for school." And the other day he went around the house asking everybody for $2. When they all turned him down, he hung paper signs on the wall saying he needed $2. "He was so annoying," Reggie says. "I gave it to him just to shut him up. But then he says to me, 'I'll do anything you want me to—right now! You want me to fold your clothes? I'll fold your clothes!' No, I told him, just stop talking." Reggie says that he's so annoying that his eighteen-year old brother with the seizures hits him.

However, Reggie did find the ten year old useful. Since the mother wouldn't give Reggie the Netflix password, Reggie had the ten year old put it in and he got it from watching him.

I ask if there's been any more talk about when they want him to leave. "Now that the mother understands me," he says, "she says she'll let me stay. But I don't want to."

Anything interesting happening at school? "I was voted Mr. University by the Texas club," he says. He says his duties are to "look nice while doing community service." I ask if he'll wear a suit for that. "Only if they make me."

College Students and Sleep

With all the concerns freshmen have—financing their education, grades, homesickness, making friends, roommates—there's one aspect of being a student that is rarely thought about. And that is sleep. Yet all one needs to do is visit morning classes at any college to see that sleep is a big issue in the life of a college student. Most students who miss their early morning classes miss them because they are in bed sleeping. Even the students who make it to class usually are sleep-deprived. Their eyelids are heavy, their heads droop forward. Like many people who work with college students, I make jokes about students sleeping in the classroom, but sleep-deprived students are no laughing matter. Students should be as concerned about how much sleep they get as they are concerned about any other issue affecting their lives as students.

Everyone knows by now that seven to eight hours of sleep is suggested for nearly every person. But that amount of sleep is even more necessary for college students. Why? When we sleep our brains move what we have learned that day from our short-term memory to our long-term memory. However, this process doesn't take place if the night's sleep is short or interrupted. Lack of sleep impairs a student's ability to retain information. Also, lack of sleep increases the likelihood that a student will be less likely to focus on preparing for tests ("Sleep Disorders Health Center").

Moreover, according to Lawrence Epstein M.D., "Sleep deprivation affects not only whether students can stay awake in class but how they perform as well." He says that after sleeping six hours or less a night for two weeks, students perform as poorly on class work as someone who has gone without sleep for forty-eight hours ("College Students"). In other words, not getting enough sleep will negatively affect a student's grades. Students who rely on pulling all-night study sessions in order to prepare for tests are more likely to have a low G.P.A. ("College Students"). The reason is that without enough sleep the brain doesn't have enough time to process and retain the information, which is a process that takes place during sleep ("Sleep Disorders").

In order for students to perform at their peak, sleep is vital. Getting enough sleep is as important as having effective study habits. Therefore any time students have activities that are interfering with their sleep, they need to ask themselves if sacrificing their grades is worth it, since ultimately, that is what sleep depravation leads to: lower grades. What I tell my students is that the best way to gauge the importance of something is to use the ten-year rule. Ten years from now what will be more important to you—the partying you did in college, the friends you hung out with in college, or the grades you earned in college? If the answer is grades, then obviously students need to do everything in their power to work towards achieving the highest grades they can. Getting enough sleep is a good place to start.

A Day in the Life of a College Student

My plan this week is to have each of the four students give a detailed schedule of their longest day of the week.

October 30

Tameka

I guess I'll have to wait until next week to get Tameka's schedule. She texts me and says she can't make it this week. She must have gotten a different work schedule this week.

Michael

Michael also texts me. He is busy and will need to reschedule for next week.

Ashley

Ashley's schedule for a Wednesday

8:30—wake up, shower, dress, then read for her history class in her room while her roommate is in class.

9:45—leave room, get to history class early so that she can get a seat up front so that she can see

11:00—English class, sit in middle of room, not so many students in this class, write an essay for punishment (someone was talking on their phone and the instructor punished the whole class, essay topic is why failure is a better teacher than success)

12:00—back to room to work on lyceum for First-Year Seminar

1:00—Math class, she sits next to girl who lives in her dorm

2:00-3:30 —run to lunch somewhere in this time, if she doesn't get there before two they sometimes close the doors and don't let her in

2:30-3:00 —in her room, scan proof for lyceum to Turn It In (she needs to prove that she went to the event, e.g. panel discussion on domestic violence, art gallery)

3:00—meeting with me

3:30—Back to room to proofread lyceum and submit it electronically by four

4:00—relaxing, taking a nap or watching Netflix—she's working her way through the nine seasons of Gray's Anatomy

6:00-8:00—do homework, write papers, study, read, sometimes she goes back to watching Gray's Anatomy

8:30-9:00—eating dinner in caf, or sometimes she stays in room and eats Raman Noodles

9:00-10:00—in room relaxing with roommate, talking, watching TV or goes down hall to watch TV with friends

10:00-12:00—studies, gets sleepy, falls asleep, if she falls asleep with her laptop open, her roommate closes it and turns it off for her

What do you think about your days? "They're a little stressful. I'm glad when they're over."

Reggie

Reggie's Wednesday schedule

7:45—wakes up, lies in bed getting his mind ready, showers, dresses, doesn't eat breakfast (not hungry)

10:00—tells the mother he's ready for her to drive him to the airport

10:30—takes the train from the airport, then the shuttle to the library

11:00—studies in the library

12:00—eats in the caf with some friends

1:00—Biology class

2:00—English class

3:00—eats again, or he finds a friend or he watches TV in the student center

4:00—comes to see me

5:00—Texas club meeting

6:00—takes shuttle to train station, train to airport where either the mother or the father picks him up. "They're usually late," he says.

7:00—Home, sometimes he eats leftovers from dinner, he talks to the kids, goes to his room, sometimes he does schoolwork but usually watches shows of Netflix. He says, "The hardest thing in my day is finding something on Netflix to watch." He has so much free time that he's watched everything he wants to see. "I watch whole seasons of shows in a couple of days," he says.

10:00-12:00—somewhere in this time he goes to bed

Thursday 8:30—"I fake get up and go to the kitchen, open the fridge and say hi to everybody," he says. Then he goes back to bed. He does this because the mother told him she doesn't like people in her house to sleep past nine.

On Tuesdays and Thursdays Reggie doesn't have classes and says he gets bored. He watches Netflix, sits outside or studies. One time he was sitting outside and the mother asked him if he goes outside to smoke because, she said, that's what people usually do when they go outside. Reggie doesn't smoke.

Reggie seems a bit dejected as he describes his schedule to me. He keeps playing with my tape dispenser, pulling off little pieces of tape and sticking them on his chair. I ask him if something's wrong. "The mother," he says. "Is the truce over?" I ask. "Yes," he says. "She told me today I had to get ready by nine. It's usually ten. She said it wasn't fair to her if I'm not ready by nine. She said, 'Whose fault is it that you're not ready at nine?' It's her fault because she hadn't said anything. She said that she just thought that one day I'd get ready at nine. She said it's not fair to her youngest son because she has to homeschool him and still drive me to the airport." She said this to him today as they drove to the airport. Reggie says he stared out his window as she spoke.

She told him that she knows that he doesn't like living under her rules, but Reggie responded by saying that everywhere you go you have to live under someone's rules. And the other day she told him again that he doesn't have to eat dinner with them. "Don't you want me to eat with you?" he said. Yesterday they didn't call him to dinner. Not until after they'd eaten did they ask him if he wanted anything. "No, I'm good," he said. Sunday they didn't bother to ask him to go to church.

At school Reggie says that he stopped hanging around with one of his friends. He says that his friends from the North aren't so friendly and that he does better with his friends from Texas. But since he's only on campus two days a week he doesn't see them that much.

Last week it seemed that Reggie felt better about his situation since he and the mother aired out their grievances and seemed to reach an understanding. This week Reggie is down. There's no other way to put it. He says, "It's going back to the way it was." One minute he tells me what a good time he had at Homecoming and the next minute he says he's lost hope in getting a co-signer for his loan and doesn't know what he's going to do for next semester.

A Day in the Life of a College Student (cont.)

November 6

Tameka's Monday Schedule

7:00—wakes up, gets ready while watching *The Jeffersons* on TV, eats breakfast in her room because the caf doesn't open till 8 o'clock

8:00—Biology

9:00—World Literature

10:00—Math

11:00-11:30—goes to caf for something to eat

11:30-2:30—She studies in her room and if she has time she takes a nap for no more than forty-five minutes (she sets her alarm clock), she says, "I hate it that I can only sleep for forty-five minutes!"

3:00-5:00—Biology lab

5:00-5:20—to caf for dinner, eats fries, hamburger or pizza or maybe she'll have them make her a sandwich

5:30-5:45—back at dorm room to put on work clothes

6:00-11:00—at work, ringing up groceries and taking items back that customers leave behind

11:00-1:40—Back to room, takes shower, eats noodles or a sandwich, TV on, she's thinking about what's due tomorrow in her classes, if something is due she does it

1:40-2:00—in this time she's in bed and falling asleep

Tuesday 7:00 a.m.—alarm wakes her up

It's obvious from her schedule why Tameka looks tired today as we talk (even though it's not Monday). She rolls her head from side to side as if trying to keep herself awake. She tells me she couldn't meet with me last week because she had to track down her manager at work and talk to him about Thanksgiving. She had hoped that they would not schedule her to work during the holiday, but she found out otherwise. She'd already spent $111 on a one-way train ticket home. "I'm not happy about this," she says, as she rocks from side to side in the chair. "I better get off for Christmas." She explains to me that she's still considered a probationary employee. She has to work for 180 days before she's taken off probation. She explains that she's a model employee and doesn't see any reason why she can't get what's called a "Student Education Leave" for Christmas.

Tameka reports that she got a 100 on her latest math test, and that everything is going fine in her World Literature class. "We've gone four weeks without a quiz," she says. "That's fine with me." In Biology she's been hoping that her professor will drop their lowest grade. "He says he'll do that if everybody does well on the next test," she says. I ask how many people are in that class. "Thirty to forty," she says, "but I think he'll drop it anyway, no matter what everyone does."

This week students are registering for their classes for next semester, so I ask some questions about next semester. I ask what she hopes will be different. Her response is about herself. She says, "I'm going to be built for all this reading. I'll be more prepared, I guess. I wasn't prepared for all this reading." She also says that she hopes she'll have a different roommate next semester, but she says, "I don't think that she's moving out."

She also tells me that she hopes that she'll get off for spring break next semester. Also, she says, "I want to join more clubs. I feel like I'm missing out. I want to be more active and hang out with friends."

Afraid that I'm intruding on her naptime, I tell Tameka I'll see her next week. "I hope you get some rest," I say.

Michael's Wednesday Schedule

7:52—wake up, "I like waking up at odd times," he says. He stays in bed until 8:12

8:13—showers, dresses

9:00—English class

10:00—Science

11:00—lunch—fried chicken Wednesday, salad, rice, pink lemonade

12:00—Science lab, "It's so long, nearly two hours," he says.

2:00—Culture and Society

3:00-6:00—nap time

6:00—Get ready to go to friend's room

6:30—in friend's room, talking, chilling, "not really doing anything"

9:30—Go to eat at caf—the late night eat—burgers, fries and Grape Fanta

10:30—Back to friend's room

11:30—out on the promenade walking around

1:00—back at his room, studies till 2 or 2:30

Thursday 9:02—wakes up for 9:25 class, "I'm always late to it," he says. "The professor just waits around for the students to arrive."

Michael says that in his math class his grade is a D. Now that he has the code for the online assignments, he plans to spend next week dedicating himself to working on his math class. In his English class Michael says that his instructor told him he did a good job with presenting an analysis of a poem to her. When I ask him what poem it was, he says, "I can't remember. Wait, I'll remember. No, I can't." He still "hates" his speech class.

I get a big surprise when I ask Michael if he's registered for his next semester classes. His face turns into a serious face. "No," he says. "I probably won't be coming back next semester." He needs $7,500. For this semester a friend from home had paid it for him but Michael says he's not going to ask that person this time. "I can't do that to them again," he says. I ask if he has a backup plan. "I'll probably go into the military, the Reserves. I'll go to basic training, make some money and then re-enroll back in school at some time," he says. I ask if getting a job now is an option in order to try to raise some money. "I've applied at American Eagle," he says. "Maybe if I show the school I'm good for the money they'll let me stay. I really want to stay here." I ask what he will do if he doesn't get a job and if he doesn't go into the military. "Then I'm never coming back," he says.

To complicate matters, his family is moving to an apartment to downsize and save money. His father still works but is sick. I ask Michael if he's told his parents about his situation. "My dad doesn't know yet," he says. "My mom does. She says she's praying for me. She doesn't want me to come back home. She wants me to stay in school."

Overall Michael says, "It's been a rough week."

Ashley

In Ashley's First-Year Seminar course they are studying financial literacy. I ask her if she practices what she's being taught. She shrugs. "Yeah, I guess," she says. In Critical Thinking she received a 100 on the latest test. About science, she says, "I don't think I took a test. Wait, did I? I don't think so." She doesn't have any grades to report in any of her other classes.

Outside of the classroom Ashley will be taking part in a leadership series. I ask her what that is. "I don't know," she says. "It sounded interesting." The Bold and Beautiful club had a sleep over at one of the senior's apartments last weekend. Eleven girls slept on the floor. "It was fun," she says. I ask what other activities the club has. "We meet three or four times a month. We had a coin drive to raise money for a dinner we're having. We're having a pageant next semester, where we'll choose Miss Bold and Beautiful. We have a dinner next month and at our general meetings we talk about upcoming events." I ask how being a member of this club has helped her. "It's helped me meet people and to get the upper classmen's perspective on how to maintain a balance between school and other stuff," she says.

Ashley says that for next semester she hopes that she doesn't have any eight o'clock classes. "I also want smaller classes," she says. "Small classes help me more, help me to focus more. But I doubt I'll get small classes."

What will you do differently? "I need to start writing stuff down," she says. "I forget to do my homework. I need to remind myself, maybe I need to get an agenda book." I ask if she could get her phone to remind her. She shrugs.

Next semester she wants to get to know people better than she does, and she wants to be more involved. Lastly, Ashley says that she doesn't "want to want to sleep as much." She says that whenever she's in her room she feels like taking a nap. She wants to stop that. "Sometimes I'm just sleeping because," she says.

As usual I ask her about her roommate. "We were arguing yesterday that I didn't respond when she called my name. I was trying to sleep and she wanted to know where the remote was for the TV. She got mad because she called my name like thirty times and I didn't say anything. She got up and turned the TV off herself. We argued in the dark for like fifteen minutes and I started saying crazy stuff like I didn't have to respond to her because of the First Amendment and stuff like that. But we couldn't take each other seriously."

Reggie

Reggie's glad that his overall grade in Biology is now 79. It's getting closer to the B he's striving for. He's also trying to get a B in English. Today in English his class debated whether or not fourteen year olds should be tried as adults. "I said no," Reggie says. "I talked about how their brain isn't mature until twenty five and their concept of morality isn't there. They don't think about it." Reggie's side won the debate and they will receive either a pass on a quiz or a pass on checking their class notes. Reggie says he has to meet with his English professor to find out about his overall grade for the class. I ask if he still finds his professor mean. He says, "She's still mean but she can't help it. She's just naturally mean. It's not her fault. She wants everyone to know it's her class." The class put her in a good mood the other day. They found out it was her birthday and they sang "Happy Birthday" to her. "It made her happy," he says. "She let us watch a movie instead of having class."

For the Texas club Reggie is in charge of coming up with ideas for the community service they plan to perform. He calls his idea the Texas Roundup. They will find a local elementary school with an after school program and they will round up food and drinks and help the students with their homework.

Without my asking, Reggie tells me that he's staying here for Thanksgiving. He isn't going home. "You mean you'll be with the family?" I ask. He rolls his eyes. "Not if I can help it. I wish we had class on Thanksgiving. I'd come," he says.

"How are things there?" I ask. He looks up at the ceiling, takes a deep breath. "You know, when it comes down to it, I guess I wouldn't change a thing," he says. "I've never laughed more. The mother is learning how ridiculous she is. I'm teaching her that. She told me that we can go back to leaving the house at ten on the days I go to school."

He has more to say about the mother. "She shoots slugs," he says.

"That's what we say back home about people who say things indirectly to you, like when they indirectly insult you," he says. "The one night she said when I was in the kitchen, 'Whoever goes into the kitchen late at night makes a lot of noise. It's too loud.' She said it like she could have been talking to anyone, but I know it was me. I'm the only one up late at night. I use the microwave. And she's jealous of my hair. She's always talking about it. It's irritating. The other day she touched it and said, 'Oh, it's thick.' I said, 'Thicker than most.' She knew I was getting her back. I was talking about her. Her hair is thinner than mine."

Reggie says he's also a bit angry that Friday it took her over an hour to pick him up from the train station. She didn't apologize, just said that one of her kids had to do something. Despite his anger, he did go to church with them Sunday and he sat next to the woman who tried to take his phone last time. This time she didn't mention anything about his phone. Reggie says this woman works for a food bank and she brought the family food for dinner, but she didn't know what the meat was so Reggie wouldn't touch it. "It looked like crunch berries," he says. "I'm not eating that, I told them. I just ate the side dishes.

"Those kids are learning from me," he says. "They're not used to someone refusing to do something. I don't always eat what they're having and I don't go to bed early like them. And I'm learning from them too," he says. He's learning about what it takes to have a big family. "They have these special nights where they do stuff. One night is Inside Picnic night where they spread newspaper on the floor and eat on the floor. It's lame but I want to participate. Sunday night is Movie Night and Thursday night is Game Night. I tried to play Monopoly with them one night but they take it too seriously," he says. "I'm like, you guys are making me mad. I couldn't deal with it."

Reggie says that he feels like the "red-headed stepchild" around them. He stands out from them and is seen as something of a rebel. "You all are so weird, I'm always thinking," he says. The fourteen-year-old girl eats everything with chopsticks. One night Reggie asked why she did that. "She was eating nachos. 'You're crazy,' I said. 'You can't eat nachos with chopsticks! Why do you have to eat everything with chopsticks?' The parents said, 'Yeah, why is that?'" Reggie said, "You all haven't wondered why until now?"

Reggie says that despite the fact that he's learning from them and they're learning from him, sometimes "I just snap." The mother called Reggie's mom to ask if Reggie had ever taken anger management classes. His mom just laughed, he says. "She thought it was funny."

High School vs. College

November 13

This week I ask the four students specific questions about college classes. I want to find out how they view them as compared to high school classes and I want to get their perspective of college classes in general.

What are the biggest differences between classes in high school and classes in college?

Tameka: "In high school they gave you a study guide. If you followed the study guide, no problem. Tests were easier in high school and there was less reading. In college if it's in the reading, the professors expect you to know it. In college you need to learn things faster."

Michael: "Freedom. You can have your phone out, can go to the bathroom or out to answer a call. You don't need to raise your hand. Classes are a little harder. In English you can't use I, we, you or contractions. In college there are a lot of lectures, no hands on teaching like in high school."

Ashley: "In college it's not a big deal if you don't come to class. No one calls your parents. If you don't come it's on you. They are more general on what their tests are on in college. In high school they give you a review date and tell you everything that will be on the test. Here you're on your own. There's no review date. Another thing that's different is that if you're late to class, some professors won't let you in or they make you wait outside and let you in eventually."

Reggie: "There's more freedom in class. If you don't want to come, no one's calling your mom. Classes in college are more relaxed, more laid back. No tests every Friday like in high school. And in college, after a semester if you're tired of a teacher you just get a different one. In high school it's a big deal to get a new teacher. You're more or less stuck with the one you got for the whole year."

What surprised you the most about college classes?

Tameka: "The movies make the college classroom look so exciting. But they're not. Some are really boring. I thought the professors would be more engaging than they are. I'm disappointed by the lack of enthusiasm from some of my professors. It's like they're saying, 'I don't want to be here any more than you do.' My friends who go to other schools say it's the same there, too."

Michael: "The students. They're all smart and educated. Here people want to come to school. It's not like that in high school. I enjoy this here."

Ashley: "The amount of work you have to do. You don't get a warming up like in high school. You just have to remember everything and do it on your own. Also, there are a lot more students in the classes. Only my English class is the same size as it was in high school. The size of college classes surprised me."

Reggie: "The classes aren't as hard as I thought they'd be. Maybe it's because I only have two classes. In middle school they told us how hard classes would be in high school. They really hyped it up, but it wasn't as hard as they said. And in high school they said how hard classes would be in college, but they're not. Although, I guess, being a part-time student is a lot easier than being a full-time student."

What do you like the most and the least about college classes?

Tameka: "I love fifty minute classes. When you have a boring professor you get out quick."

Michael: "I like the freedom and the students. I like to see African Americans educated, but we need to get more black males in college. There's something wrong. What I don't like is my speech class. It's too late in the day and I'm not learning anything."

Ashley: "You can pick your own schedule, and I like it that when classes are cancelled you don't have to stay in the class with a sub. You can just go back to your room. I don't like Tuesday and Thursday classes because they're an hour and fifteen minutes. I do like that some of the classes are discussion-based. I also like it that they make you become more responsible in college. It makes me more responsible with what I spend my time on. I don't like it though that professors don't give extra credit and I don't like lecture-based classes, like my Critical Thinking class."

Reggie: "I like it that the professors ask you what you think and that they use personal experiences to illustrate points. It's like you don't even realize you're learning. What I like the least are my professors' bad moods. When my Biology professor is in a bad mood she doesn't get up to talk; she just sits down and gives a slide show."

Daily, how much time did you put into studying for a high school class and how much time do you put into studying for a college class?

Tameka: "In high school, total for all my classes, maybe thirty minutes a day if tests were coming up. In college, it depends on the class. For World Literature I might spend two hours a day on that class."

Michael: "In high school I only studied for two classes—AP lit. and Science. Those classes were a killer. I spent three hours each night on them. Here I also don't study for every class every night. I haven't really started studying for math yet. I've been a slacker. For the most part it depends what's going on that determines what I study, like if I have a test coming up."

Ashley: "Honestly, I really didn't study in high school. In college I spend thirty to forty minutes for each class every day. In high school they spent time in class making sure the stuff got in your brain. In college you have to do that on your own."

Reggie: "I didn't study in high school unless I was in trouble. If a teacher called my mom or report cards were coming, then I might pull out a book. I didn't understand the concept of studying. In college, every day I spend about an hour to an hour and a half on each class."

Are you learning in your classes?

Tameka: "In First-Year Seminar I'm learning a lot about the school. The professor is very engaging. In World Literature I have to learn. She's really making us work for our grades. And I like some of the works we read, like Frederick Douglass and "Diary of a Madman." In Biology I don't feel like I'm learning yet because it's so boring. And that's my major. I guess I haven't gotten to the good stuff yet. I am learning in History and speech."

Michael: "Science no, speech no, math is a review, English yes. I'm learning in that class. I'm learning how to write. She's hard and that's helping me. In Culture and Society I'm learning about family values, how men are when they aren't the breadwinners and what women have to do when they are the breadwinners. I'm not learning anything in First-Year Seminar. I really wanted to learn in speech. I want to learn public speaking. Speech was supposed to be my best class. I'm frustrated."

Ashley: "In history, I'm learning about the world and Africa. I'm learning stuff I didn't know about Africans. That's important to me because it's part of my history. In Pre-professional I'm learning stuff that pertains to my profession, teaching. In English I'm learning to write better. For Critical Thinking, I'm not sure how I'm supposed to use it in everyday life. And First-Year Seminar—I don't get that class. I don't know what we're supposed to be learning."

Reggie: "In Biology, I learned about hair and genetics. I learned who loses their hair and who doesn't. I'm interested in that. For English, I'm not sure I'm learning. I'm not learning to write better. Maybe if we understood the assignments better, if she gave us an example we could use."

A visit from Reggie wouldn't be complete without a report about a recent incident with the mother. Reggie sleeps in the basement and lately the weather has gotten cold. Since Reggie's from Texas he's used to heat. The family has a little space heater and Reggie asked the father if he could use it in his room. At first the father was worried about it starting a fire, but he told Reggie that he could use it. The next day the mother spoke to Reggie about his asking for the heater. She said, "We were too generous with you when you first came here. We bought you a mattress and a rack for your clothes. Anything else is extra. I don't think it was okay for you to tell us you're cold. Why would you expect me to care about you being cold? That's not my problem, not my responsibility."

"When she said she was too generous I said, 'Why would you apologize for being nice? That doesn't make sense.' What she was mad about was that her kids wouldn't have asked for a heater if they were cold. They'd just not say anything and freeze. She says she's raising them like it's the 1950s and that her kids have different values from me. I was so mad. I told her to just treat me like an adult. I'm eighteen. I'm an adult. She expects me to act like a kid, like I'm one of her kids. But I told her, I'm not a kid. I told her I'm old enough to kill her and go to prison for it. I was so mad. She just doesn't know how stupid she sounds."

Thanksgiving

November 20

Tameka

Tameka texts me that she's working and can't see me.

Michael

This week Michael says he isn't going to leave school. "I'm gonna find a way to stay," he says. "There's no way I can leave." He's found a job. Starting soon he will be working at the Armani Exchange. He will be working about twenty-five hours a week.

When I tell Michael that today I want to ask him about his fellow students and friends, he gets excited. His smile increases in size and he tucks his legs under him in his chair and sits on them. He tells me that there really isn't a big difference between the students he saw in high school and the ones in college. "They're childish and talkative," he says. He says there isn't much of a difference because "we're transitioning and it isn't as smooth as you'd expect."

Michael says in high school he had about twenty five friends. About his friends, he says, "They were fun, ambitious, sentimental at times and were motivational. All of them went on to college except for three."

Those three went into the armed services. In college he has twelve friends. "They are different," he says. "And I can see them as long-term friends. They motivate each other, let each other know about acting casting calls and dance casting calls. They help each other and look for opportunities for each other. They're an emotional group. We do all kinds of stuff together. We've known each other since January from social media."

I ask him what he's learned about having a roommate. He says, "People are nasty and inconsiderate." His roommate talks on the phone really loudly when Michael is trying to watch TV. "Last night I turned the volume on my TV all the way up to 100 because he was so loud." I ask if the roommate said anything or changed his behavior. "No," he says. "And I didn't turn my TV down. I fell asleep with it like that. When I woke up in the morning, I thought, Wow, that's really loud."

Has having a roommate helped you to learn anything about yourself? "I didn't think I was such a clean freak," he says. "I didn't know I was this clean. I've learned that I just have to clean up. I'm really a clean person."

We close with Michael telling me that he did poorly on a special pop quiz in Culture and Society—he got 20/50—and that he won't be going home for Thanksgiving because of his job. I ask him what he thinks of that. "I'm fine with it," he says.

Ashley

Ashley says that her fellow students in college are more opinionated than in high school. "They don't care if they're rude to the professors," she says. "They just speak their mind." She says that in one of her classes there is a student who will say comments out loud when she doesn't agree with something the professor says. Another way college students are different from high school students, she says, is that they are unprepared for class. "Here nobody reads the work," she says. "In high school we had quizzes on what we read. Here we don't have them." Therefore the students don't see a reason to read assignments.

Finally, Ashley says that in college students come and go in the classroom as they please. "They come late to class or they don't come at all. They don't seem to care," she says. And in college students don't try to hide their phones. "In high school if they saw your phone they took it," she says. "You had to pay to get it back. Here the professors mostly don't care. Except for my history professor. You get points taken off your grade if you use your phone in that class."

About friends, Ashley says that she had a good ten to fifteen in high school. She rode together with them, danced with them. "Some of them were really funny," she says. They all went on to college. Here there are about six students she considers friends. "We have good conversations," she says. "We always laugh when we're together." One of her favorite things to do with them is to move from room to room watching *Love and Hip Hop*. They keep their doors open, yell back and forth and visit each others' rooms when it's playing.

Ashley says that what she's learned about having a roommate is that she just can't do whatever she wants. "I have to consider what she's doing," she says. "I usually have my head phones on when I leave the room and I used to slam the door when my roommate was sleeping. I couldn't hear it. I used to wake her up. Now I make sure I don't slam the door." Another thing she's learned is that "I really hate taking out the trash," she says. "Last night my roommate and I were arguing about who needs to take out the trash. I'm stubborn. I don't want to do it. I don't like it."

As for her grades, Ashley says that so far she's getting an A in Critical Thinking, B in English and History, A in Pre-professional Seminar, and in First-Year Seminar, she says "I don't know. I got 60 on the last lyceum. I have to make that up."

Ashley will be flying home with her roommate for Thanksgiving. Her birthday is the day after Thanksgiving this year. Her family will be taking her out Friday and her friends will be taking her out Saturday.

Reggie

Like Tameka, Reggie texts me that he can't make it this week. He didn't say why.

End of Semester

December 4

Tameka

For the last interview of the semester, besides asking about what they did for Thanksgiving, I want to ask reflective questions about their first semester at college, to give them an opportunity to assess the beginning of their college career.

Tameka says that on the Wednesday before Thanksgiving she had off from Walmart. "I just slept all day," she says. "And I watched some TV." She needed the sleep because the next day, Thanksgiving, she worked two shifts. First she worked from seven in the morning to noon, then from four to nine. "It was busy," she says. "There were about twenty five cops there and they had the people in lines outside in the parking lot. TVs and iPads were on sale. We had thirty-two inch TVs on sale for $98. So many people." For lunch her manager took Tameka out to the Golden Corral because she too is not from the area and didn't have any family to celebrate Thanksgiving with.

Compared to Thanksgiving, Tameka says Black Friday was slow. Since we last spoke, Tameka says she received good news from her boss. "They're letting me take a thirty-day vacation so I can go home for Christmas," she says. "I feel good about that. I think staying for Thanksgiving and not going home made it worth it to get Christmas off." However, when I ask her what she'll do at home on her vacation, I get a surprise. Thinking that she'll say sleep or relax, I ask the question with confidence at the answer. "I'll work my job at home," she says. "At Bojangles." "You'll be working more?" I say. "Yeah," she says. "I'll also spend time with my family and my boyfriend and my very few friends. I'm looking forward to seeing them all. This will be my first time home. My brother sent me a Christmas list of things he wants. He said, 'You have the money. You work at Walmart.'"

Besides making money, Tameka has gotten something else of value from working at Walmart. "Working there just makes me want to work harder in school," she says. The other day she got into something of an argument with a customer. The customer got angry at her and spoke to the manager about Tameka. Before he spoke to the manager, the customer said to Tameka, "You won't be here long." Says Tameka, "And I thought to myself, you're right. I won't. This is why I'm going to school."

In her classes, Tameka reports receiving a perfect score on a Biology lab test and a 64 on a First-Year Seminar test. "The test was on more than what he told us to study," she says. "I'll study hard for the final and bring my grade back up. The same questions that were on the test will be on the final. I won't get them wrong again." World Literature has been the class that has given her the most trouble. Tameka says that lately the class hasn't been meeting because her instructor had a car accident and has had to cancel some classes. "I'm hoping for an A in that class," Tameka says.

As for her first semester in college, Tameka describes it as "fast. It went by so fast," she says. "The end just sneaks up on you."

Now that you've been here for a semester, what do you think about college? "I think it's as good as you make it. It's worth how much you put into it. It's more than going to class. It's about learning ways to find opportunities," she says.

What mistakes did you make? "Not preparing myself over the

summer," she says. "I should have been reading up on my major Biology to have a background in it. Also, I didn't study enough."

What did you do right? "My schedule. Having classes back to back really helped me with time. Another thing was talking to my professors. I got stuff straightened out with them and I showed them that I'm working hard in my classes."

What will you do differently next semester? "I'll read my Biology textbook. I've only been skimming it. I need to be more proactive. I got to do stuff like write in the margins."

What did you learn about being a college student? "The professors don't spoonfeed you. They don't baby you," she says. Also, about professors, she says she's learned that "professors might be in their office during office hours or they might not be."

Michael

For Thanksgiving Michael went to Hooters with two friends. He didn't go home because he worked at his new job, the Armani Exchange. As usual Michael was all smiles and full of enthusiasm despite the fact that he had a good amount of bad news to report. I'll start with his grades. In his English class the project that he worked on and presented to the class, about how the media portrays men, did not go well. His instructor told Michael that it was too long and "that the facts weren't accurate." "She also told me that I missed too many classes during the semester. But I only missed two. The other students said they'd back me up. She only takes roll when she wants to. I'm getting an F in that class. I'm flunking," he says. The only good news he got from his classes was from his speech class. "The ending of that class was great," he says. "I did a really good job on my last speech. It was on why there should be drug testing in the workplace. I got 135 out of 150. That was better than my first speech. I feel better about that class now."

Michael got a dose of bad news from home. First, his mother lost one of her jobs. She got laid off from the power plant. The brother who is also in college lost his job too. And his oldest brother was sent to prison for driving without a license. On top of that, his father is still sick. Because of all this bad news, the last thing Michael wants to do is cause any more problems. His situation was stressing his mother out. "I don't want her to be stressed out over how I'll pay for school," he says. "I've made up my mind, I'm going into the National Guard. They'll pay me ten thousand a year for school. I'll go to basic training and AIT and I'll be back home by June. After that I just need to go one weekend a month and two weeks in the summer. I'll come back here to school next fall. God has a plan, and I think this is it."

I ask him how his friends at school took the news. "This was a hard decision for me," he says. "When I told my friends they cried and walked away. That was tough. I've been trying to spend as much time with them as I can before I go home." I also ask him if he's ready for basic training. "I don't know," he says. "I won't be able to use my phone for months, or a computer. I don't know how I'll handle that."

Even with all that has happened to him during his first semester at college, Michael uses the word "great" to describe his college experience. "I had a great time, met great people; …everything about the school is great except the price. It's a great school," he says. Overall he says about college in general, "It's what I thought it would be. It has its upsides and it can be very stressful."

As for his mistakes, he says that failing English was a big mistake he made. "I didn't put forth my best effort," he says. "Also, another mistake was limiting myself to the city. I haven't been out of the city to see all that the state has to offer."

What he did right, he says, was meeting great people. "I had a good time, I did some studying, made my family proud. I made the right decision." I ask him what he'll do differently when he comes back. "I will actually study and take classes more seriously."

What did he learn about being a college student? "You have to give and take and make up for the mistakes you made when you were younger. My dad always told me to save my money, but I didn't and now wish I had. My mom said the best way to lose friends is to live with them." I ask him if that's what happened with his first roommate. First they were friends, then roommates, and then they didn't like each other. Michael nods. "Yeah," he says.

What will you miss? "My friends," he says.

What would you have done differently? "Study," he says. "That's it. Studying is what I would do differently."

Ashley

Ashley drags her feet into my office. She looks sleepy and a little off. She tells me she is sleepy and she has a cold. After we talk, she says she's going to go back to her room and nap. She perks up, however, when I ask her what she did for Thanksgiving. She and her roommate flew home to Maryland. The day after Thanksgiving was her birthday and her mom told her to wake up early and to dress warmly. They were going somewhere for her birthday but her mother said it was a surprise and wouldn't tell her where. Ashley did as her mother said, got in the car and noticed there were snacks and sandwiches. Joining them were her aunt and two cousins. They wouldn't tell her where they were going so she slept some of the way. "When I saw signs for the New Jersey Turnpike I realized where we were going," she says. "We spent the day in New York shopping and eating," she says. "It was great."

On Saturday her father took her to her first NHL hockey game. They went to Washington D.C. to see the Capitals play. "My dad is a hockey fan," she says. "We sat up high. There were a lot of people there. It was funner than basketball games," she says.

The word Ashley uses to describe her first semester at college is "different." She says, "It's different from what people said it was going to be. They said college is fun and that you meet people all the time. That's true but they don't tell you about the work and the responsibility you have," she says. "Also, I'd describe my first semester as unique since I came here with my best friend."

Describing what she thinks about college, she says, "College is fun but it's hard at the same time. You have to find a balance between schoolwork and fun and knowing when you've had enough fun. You can't try to be like everybody else. You have to realize that somebody is paying for this whether you go to class or not."

Ashley says that the mistake she made her first semester was putting off her work and staying up too late which made getting up in the morning difficult. Another mistake she made is "thinking people have had the same upbringing as me and that they will act like me." She says that there are a lot of students who don't show respect to the professors the way she thinks they should. "Some students are really rude to the professors."

The thing she did right was to go to all of her classes. "Well, most of my classes. I also chose my friends wisely," she says. "I hear stories about people who didn't choose wisely. They have problems."

Next semester Ashley says, "I'm going to be more in tune with everything. I came here thinking I was going to transfer and that gave me the wrong mentality. I need to change that thinking in order to be more successful." I ask her what she thinks of the school now. "I'm growing to love it," she says.

What Ashley has learned about being a student is that "You have to rely on yourself. I can't expect other people to do what I need to do myself," she says.

For Christmas break, Ashley will be flying home. She won't be working over the break. Instead she plans on going to New York to see the ball drop on New Year's and she plans on sleeping more.

Reggie

Reggie says that he wanted to go home for Thanksgiving but the weather was bad so he had to stay. "I made myself sick I was so upset," he says. "My head hurt, my stomach hurt, I felt rotten." He spent Thanksgiving at the house with the family. The husband made chicken wings that Reggie says were really good. They didn't have Thanksgiving dinner until Sunday night. "I've been trying to spend time with them since I'm leaving soon," he says. "The mother kept asking me weird questions while we ate," he says. "Like did you watch Disney movies when you were young? Did you watch cartoons?" She thinks, Reggie says, that he was let on his own without guidance when he was a child. "She wants her kids to see me as strange."

The mother has also been emailing Reggie's mom, asking when he's leaving, when she's coming to pick him up. "My mom doesn't know why she isn't calling her. She's always called before. My mom is a little mad at her." The mother is asking Reggie when his finals are. "She wants to find out exactly when I'm finished. She's bugging me about when my mom's coming to get me," he says. "She keeps asking a whole bunch of questions because she likes to be in control and so she likes to know everything."

Otherwise, Reggie says that everything had been going fine with him and the mother until the other day when the narcoleptic study scheduled for the youngest daughter was cancelled. The study was set up so that the doctors could determine what medication to put her on. The mother wasn't happy about the cancellation. "She was mad and she took it out on me. She didn't talk to me for two days." Says Reggie about the daughter's narcolepsy, "The only time she seems to have narcolepsy is in church when her father's preaching."

I ask Reggie what he's learned about living with the family. He says, "that I hate living with people. I'm not having four kids, maybe two." They did teach him some positive things however. "I've never seen a husband and a wife together and kids loving their father. I also learned some parenting techniques."

"Twenty years from now," I ask, "what will you say about this experience? Will you present it in a funny way?" Reggie laughs. In a joking manner, he says, "When I was a freshman in college, let me tell you . . ." Then he changes his tone. "There was no concern for me," he says. "I went from being an only child to a big family—I wouldn't wish it on anybody," he says. "I lost friends and I had to depend on other people more. I didn't think it would be like that. My grandmother told me that the mother was crazy. She was right—she is crazy."

Reggie says he is not going to miss the conversations with the mother. The other day they got on the topic of what it would be like for Reggie's mom if he were to die before her. "I'm my mom's world," he says. "Without me my mom would die." The mother disagreed. "No, she wouldn't. Your mother would be fine without you," she said to Reggie. Reggie says he doesn't know what it's going to be like when his mother comes to pick him up. His experience with the mother has changed his mom's relationship with her. "My mom doesn't like her now," Reggie says.

Reggie can't come up with a word to describe his first semester in college. "I wouldn't say it was good or bad," he says. "I won't know till I'm older if I made the right decision to pack up and come. I had to mature a lot. I learned a lot about independence and patience. Academically, I learned how to balance things," he says.

He's also learned about professors, specifically his English professor.

"I really do like her," he says. "She's a black woman with a capital B. You need to work around her mood swings and that will make your life easier. If you learn what she's teaching, you get more out of this class. You can't think you will run the class," he says.

I ask him about mistakes he made. Was coming here without a co-signer a mistake? At first he says, "Could be, I don't know yet." Then he says, "I don't think it was a mistake."

What did you do right? "I handled myself well with friends that caused me problems. I just removed myself to avoid conflict," he says. "In the past I would have tried to talk to them. I would have gotten mad if they said something wrong and I would have gotten physical with them."

What will you do differently next semester? "I won't accept no," he says. "I learned that you don't have to always accept no. I learned that from working with financial aid. Had I been more aggressive maybe I could have enrolled sooner and maybe even full-time."

Reggie says that what he's learned about being a college student is that you need to have your priorities straight. "You have to be organized and you have to remember why you're in college," he says. "You're not enrolled just to be here. You're here for your classes."

Reggie tells me that he won't be coming back here next semester. He's transferring to a public HBCU in Texas. He'll save some money, and hopefully raise his G.P.A., get scholarships and come back here in a year. With his leaving in mind, I ask what he'll miss. "I'll miss not being recognized," he says. "I'll miss the people I've met. Except for the family. I won't miss them at all—no," he says.

I ask, if looking back, he'd have done anything differently. "I would have gone into the family's house differently—I wish I'd never got to know that side of the family. I wish I could have stayed on campus."

The last thing Reggie says to me in our last interview is "I'm just ready to leave that house."

Why Students Leave School

According to *The Journal of Blacks in Higher Education*, as a whole, the college graduation rate for African Americans is forty-two percent, which is lower than the rate for other minorities. For black women the rate is forty-six percent and for black men thirty-five percent ("Black Students' College"). The question is why is the rate so low? Why do more black students drop out of college than graduate?

There are many reasons. Often each student who drops out has his or her own unique reason. However, there are two primary reasons students drop out. The first is financial. Because many African American students come from low-income families, the pressure to pay for college often becomes too much to bear and they are forced to leave school. Moreover, low-income families usually have few books in the home and don't stress reading, which is vital to student success, and low-income families have parents who did not attend college and who are unable to prepare their children intellectually and emotionally for college ("Black Students' College"). In other words, having limited resources not only challenges students while in college but also before.

Lack of money, however, is only a part of the problem. After financial difficulties, the second reason African American students drop out of college at a high rate is because many don't know how to be a college student. As a result, they perform poorly in the classroom and become academically disqualified—they flunk out.

Understanding how to be a student involves knowledge that students from households without a college graduate often don't possess. First-time college students face challenges that they aren't always prepared for—how to effectively study for tests, how much time to put into each class outside of the classroom, how to write effective papers and how to make use of professors' office hours. In high school these issues rarely came up and didn't seem to have an impact on the students' grades.

How to be a college student includes how to manage time away from the classroom. With the new freedom that first-time college students enjoy, extra-curricular activities can become more important to the student than schoolwork. Students discover that there are so many campus activities to partake in and so many new and interesting people to hang out with that they don't realize that they need to create a balance between schoolwork and fun. When fun becomes a priority, grades suffer.

Many students come to mind when I think of students who had trouble striking a balance between schoolwork and extra-curricular activities. A recent example is a student I taught in Freshman Composition I. She was not the best writer but she put in the time and effort to improve her writing, often spending time with me in my office going over papers in progress. She worked hard and got an A in the class. However, in Freshman Composition II she wasn't the same student. She didn't have me look at drafts of her papers. She handed in low quality papers and seemed distracted in class--when she came to class. She missed quite a few. Midway through the semester, after she received a D for her mid-term grade, I asked her what was going on. She told me that she was involved in so many organizations and activities that they were taking the place of schoolwork. I told her she needed to make a change. She agreed, but I saw little evidence of a change. Her papers were still of poor quality and she did not seek my help. She managed to eke out a C in the class. All I could do was shake my head and think, what a shame.

How to be a college student also includes having the mindset of a college student. Not thinking like a college student has led many a student astray. Again, it is a question of priorities. I once had a colleague say to me, "When I have students who are more concerned with showing off their body parts, I know those are students who probably aren't going to make it." Another colleague recently remarked to me that she sees students with $500 hair weaves who tell her that they don't have money to buy their books for their classes. What my colleagues are getting at is that students whose first priority is to attract attention to their physical appearance—to the superficial, to hair weaves, cleavage, muscles—usually are students whose focus is not on their schoolwork, on the things of the mind. This is the reason some colleges don't allow their students to display their underwear or to dress for class as if going to the club. Students who are more concerned about the way they look over gaining knowledge aren't thinking like college students.

Furthermore, students who are more concerned with their phones than listening to the professor or paying attention to what is taking place in the classroom don't have the mindset needed for college. When students who struggled mightily to get into college and to pay for college sit in their classrooms just so they can play with their phones, those students aren't thinking, or acting, like college students. They are too distracted from what should be the most important event in their day—attending class. Their priorities are out of line, and students who lack the priorities needed to succeed in college will likely find themselves struggling and could eventually be forced to leave school, as, unfortunately, is so often the case. There are so many college dropouts out in the world who look back and say, "If only I'd had my priorities straight when I was in college, I'd have my diploma now."

Final Grades

Below are the final first semester grades for each student. On the left is the grade the student predicted he or she would receive, and on the right is the grade the student earned.

Tameka

	Grade predicted	Grade earned
Biology	A	A
First-Year Seminar	A	A
History	A	A
Speech	A	A
Algebra	A	A
World Literature	A	A

Michael

	Grade predicted	Grade earned
English	A	D
First-Year Seminar	A	C
Algebra II	A	D
Earth Science	A	C
Culture and Society	A	A
Speech	A	B

Ashley

	Grade predicted	Grade earned
Pre-Professional Seminar	A	A
English	A	A
History	B	B
Pre-Calculus	A	A
Critical Thinking	B	A
First-Year Seminar	A	A

Reggie

	Grade predicted	Grade earned
Biology	A	B
English	B	B

Spring Semester

Even before I started this project, I had anticipated that at least one of the students I interviewed would not return for the Spring semester. Experience told me that one of the four students would either discover that he or she couldn't afford college or would do so poorly that dropping out seemed like the best option. I did not, however, anticipate losing two of the four students. Since that is the case, I have decided that I will make some changes in the format of the second half of this book. To take the place of Michael and Reggie, I have asked twelve students in my College Composition II class to sit for an interview with me in order to assess their freshman experience so far. I plan to ask them questions that will give the reader a good sense of the backgrounds of these students as well as who they are as students. I will ask them what they did right as freshmen and what they did wrong and what they will do differently this semester. I will also interview four seniors to help put the freshman year in perspective. Moreover, in order to get their view of freshmen and the freshman year, I plan to interview professors from various departments who teach freshmen. My thinking is that professors who work with freshmen will be able to shed light on what it takes to be a successful student. Finally, I will talk to a financial aid representative and a school psychologist.

I think it best as well to change slightly the interview schedule for Tameka and Ashley. Now that the newness of being a freshman has worn off and they are settled into being college students, weekly interviews are more than likely not going to reveal as much as they did in the first semester. I will have Tameka and Ashley meet with me on a bi-weekly basis to assess their college life in their second semester of college. All told, I believe that the new voices and those of the familiar will further articulate the life of a freshman at an HBCU.

A quick note on Reggie. He texted me today—the first day of classes at my school and I assume at his—to tell me that he is at his new school in Texas and that "Everything seems to be going good for now." I told him to keep me updated.

New Classes

January 22

Tameka

Tameka worked twenty-five hours a week as a cashier at Bojangle's while home for Christmas break. When she wasn't working, she visited her family and hung out with friends and her boyfriend. "It was good to get away from here," she says. At home, her mother lifted her curfew, and she took advantage of that by staying over at her friend's house until four or five in the morning. "I'd fall asleep on my friend's sofa," Tameka says. "I loved not having a curfew."

Since this was her first time home since leaving for school in August, her family had a lot of questions for her. They wanted to know if school was difficult. "Some classes," she answered. Were you active on campus? "Not really, I work a lot." How do you work and get straight A's? "I don't know." Is the food good? "Some days, mainly Wednesdays and Fridays when they serve chicken and fish." About the food, Tameka informs me that since she entered school with twelve credits, she is now classified as a sophomore, which means she doesn't have to buy the full meal plan, saving her $1,500.

Her family had other questions for her. How's your roommate? "We bump heads sometimes." How do you maintain your relationship with your boyfriend? "He just has to deal with it. I talk to him every night. If he wants me he just has to make a sacrifice." Tameka tells me that at home her boyfriend followed her everywhere she went. I ask if she wears the pants in the relationship. "He thinks he does, but everyone knows I do," she says.

Tameka says she had a great time at home with her brother and sister. "We acted like I never left," she says. "We acted like little kids, pushing each other off the bed." For Christmas presents, Tameka got her brother a fifth-generation iPad and a game for his Xbox. She got her sister a North Face jacket and a pair of Ugg boots.

It wasn't easy to leave home, Tameka says. "I wasn't ready to come back to school. It felt like I was moving to school all over again. Everyone was crying—my mom, me, my family. My mom drove me back. There was lots of crying," she says. And since she's been back, Tameka's done a lot of sleeping. She doesn't start back up at Walmart until February, so she's using this time to get the sleeping in that she will lose out on once she's working again.

This semester Tameka is taking Critical Thinking, History, Biology II, Pre-calculus, the second part of First-Year Seminar and French. She's excited about taking French. It's the first time she's taken a foreign language other than Spanish, which she took in high school. In all her classes, Tameka expects to receive an A. However, from what she can tell about Critical Thinking so far, she thinks she might have some difficulty getting an A in that class. The thing that most excites her this semester is, as she says, "No English classes. Yah!" "So you won't miss World Lit.?" I say. "No!" she replies.

What Tameka would like to remain the same this semester from last semester are her good grades and her ambition and drive to do well. What she hopes will be different is, first, to improve her relationships with other students. "I still haven't found that best friend yet," she says. Second, she hopes to improve her study habits and she'd like to read more.

I ask her how she's different at the beginning of this semester compared to the beginning of last semester. "I know what I'm getting myself into," she says. "I'm more adjusted." She is still concerned though about her shyness. "When I walk into a room I think that everyone is staring at me," she says. "I hate it when on the first day the professor makes us introduce ourselves. I do it quickly then sit down."

As for joining organizations, Tameka will still be in the Biology club and plans on joining the Pre-professional Health Society. Her First-Year Seminar professor told her to join. They will help out at health clinics.

What do you look forward to this semester? "I look forward to final exams and getting to summer break," she says. "I miss my family and my boyfriend. I won't get to go home at spring break. The way I see it, if I do well in my classes, my reward is getting to go home."

What are you not looking forward to? "Getting less sleep when I start working," she says. "And tests. I'm not looking forward to tests."

Ashley

During Christmas break Ashley didn't go to New York as she had hoped she would. "I just stayed home for break," she says. "During the week I was home and on the weekends I went out with my friends who were home from college. We had a lot of good laughs," she says. "We compared our college experience." Ashley also got caught up on her sleep, getting at least eight hours a night. She says that the best Christmas presents she received were a pair of boots from her parents and a necklace from her grandmother. "It's an angel necklace," she says, "because my grandmother says I'm her angel."

Even though Ashley had visited home during last semester, her family still had questions for her about college. Do you like it? "Yeah." Do you party all the time? "Sometimes." What are your classes like? "They're long and sometimes they're boring, sometimes not, depends on the day." How's your roommate? "She's fine."

I ask her if she was ready to come back to school. "I didn't have a car on the weekdays," she says. "I had to share with my mom and she needed it for work. So during the weekdays I was ready to go back to school, but on the weekends I got to use the car. On the weekends I wanted to stay home."

Ashley expects to earn A's in Biology, the second half of First-Year Seminar, Pre-Calculus II and Speech. She's hesitant to say she'll get an A in English because so far her class doesn't have an instructor and she isn't sure what the instructor will be like, but if she had to guess about her grade, she guesses she'll get an A. She says about her Physics class, "I'll probably drop it. It's too much. I'm bored to tears. If I do keep it, I'll probably get a B."

So far, the classes that excite her are Biology and Pre-Calculus. "It's more the professors than the classes," she says. "Those two professors actually seem to care about what you're doing."

Ashley says what she hopes will be different this semester is that she gets more sleep. What she hopes will be the same is that she can build off of the relationships started with people in her dorm. When I ask her how she's different from the beginning of last semester, she says, "I'm doing things for myself now. I'm not calling my mom to help me figure things out. Like last semester when I was having problems with Student Accounts. I called my mom for help. Now, I can handle stuff like that on my own."

Another way she is different is that "I'm more open to people now. I'm more comfortable talking to people like in my classes," she says.

This semester Ashley plans on joining the Woman's Leadership Council. "I saw a flyer for it," she says. "It sounds good." Ashley has also signed up to be an Orientation Guide. "It looks like fun," she says. "You get to meet incoming freshmen and the other guides," she says.

When I ask her what she looks forward to this semester, Ashley says,

"I don't know. Spring Break?" She shrugs. What do you least look forward to? "The work," she says. "I know it only gets harder." I ask her if she's up for the challenge. "Always," she says. "I want my degree."

Francine

Francine is a Mass Media major with a concentration in Public Relations. She is from Queens, New York and comes from a family with two brothers and parents who are familiar with college. Her mother attended but dropped out, and her father received his Associate's degree. Her oldest brother is a high achiever who has his Master's degree. Her father works human resources for the government and her mother is an office manager at the high school Francine attended. Her parents separated when Francine was sixteen. She says that their separation "caused me problems."

Because of the separation of her parents, Francine says, "I didn't really care about high school. I was a bully in high school. I was bullied and I bullied people." On top of this she also had a sick grandmother she worried about while in high school. These problems contributed to a grade point average that she is less than proud of—2.78.

Francine was determined not to let her problems follow her to college. She changed her ways. "In high school I barely studied," she says. "Maybe twenty minutes a night." Her first semester of college she made it a point to be better organized, making to-do lists. She says, "Every week I made a list of everything I had to do for the week and I did it." One of the things she did was study more. Her effort netted her four A's and two B's.

Her good grades are something to be proud of; however, Francine says that earning good grades was not something she felt comfortable sharing with her college friends. "I saw good grades as a reason to be ashamed," she says. "I was afraid I wouldn't fit in." The friends she made last semester didn't earn good grades and so she didn't tell them about her grades. What Francine wants to do differently this semester is make friends with students who also have good grades. She says, "I want people that when they hear what my grades are they aren't jealous because they get good grades too."

Another change Francine plans to make in her second semester of college is not to go to class tired. "No more Thirsty Thursdays," she says. "They made getting up for Friday classes too hard. I shouldn't do that this semester."

College has changed Francine in other ways besides getting better grades. "I've learned that there are certain things I can't fight like I tried to in high school," she says. For example, last semester she nearly got involved in three fights with her suitemates. "I'm a strong-willed person," she says, "and when I heard my suitemates telling lies about my friend I almost went after them." She stopped herself each time by listening to her mother's voice in her head: "If you hit this girl and you come home, it will be me and you." Francine says, "My mom can scream her lungs out and make you regret what you did."

Nearly getting in those fights is what Francine says is the worst thing that happened to her last semester. The best thing was her G.P.A. She smiles broadly when she says it: "I got a 3.75."

What Francine likes most about college is the freedom. "I don't have someone telling me what to do like a parent," she says. "College is my time to enjoy myself and explore everything." What she likes least is the ratio of males to females. She is also troubled by the attitude of the male students. "They act like they don't think they can pass," she says. "I have a brother who dropped out and had a child at a young age and he keeps making mistakes all the time," she says. "When I see guys here like that I push them to do better, to be like my other brother with the

Master's degree. I tell them to think they can make it through college. I want to help them. I believe in them. I want to take that role."

I ask Francine what her biggest conflict is in college. "I'm the biggest conflict," she says. "My old self, being the bully, getting rid of my inner-bully."

What motivates you? "My mom and my brother,"(the one with the Master's degree). She says, "I have to get my M.A. by at least twenty three like him. And then I want to outdo him. I want to get my Ph.D."

I ask her why many other students aren't as motivated as her, why they don't make it through their freshman year. She says, "Lack of positive enforcement. They hang out with the cool people instead of the ones who want to do good. They're told it's okay to screw up their freshman year. It gets in their head."

Francine says she relies on her mom for positive reinforcement. "I talk to my mom every day. She tells me she loves me."

Francine's advice for incoming freshmen is to "surround yourself with people who have the same positive goals as you, and don't let the party scene become everything you do."

Bailey

Bailey is a Psychology major from Atlanta. She would like to pursue her Master's in Education Counseling. She's an only child. Her father passed away when she was little. Her mother re-married. Her stepfather works at a warehouse, and her mother, who has a B.A., hasn't worked for three years because of a serious medical condition.

A good student in high school, Bailey achieved a 3.5 G.P.A. and graduated 29th out of 427 students. In fact, the word she uses to describe herself when she was a high school student is "scholar."

Unfortunately, her good grades in high school didn't transfer to her first semester grades in college. "I thought I would get all A's and B's," she says. She did receive one of each, but she also received three C's and one D. "I was so disappointed," she says.

There are possible reasons for her low grades, yet Bailey can't put her finger on the culprit. She works at Kroger as a cashier, and, at the beginning of last semester, she was working up to thirty hours a week. When she told her boss that she couldn't work that many hours, her boss got her down to sixteen hours a week. She was also on the stroll team for her dorm and that often got in the way of studying.

Bailey offers two other possible reasons for why she didn't do as well as she expected. The first is that she says her courses were much harder at the end of the semester than they were at the beginning. "At the end of the semester, my professors gave us one big test after another," she says. For Bailey, big tests are a problem, which is her second possible reason for her low grades. "I have test anxiety," she says, "and I don't do well on big tests. I really struggle with them and then to have them count so much was hard for me."

This semester she says that there are several things she's going to do to improve her grades. The first is to be more organized. The second is to study more. "This semester I'm going to study an hour a day for each class." Further, she says that while she did do some things well last semester, such as turning her work in on time and participating in class, this semester in math class she needs to take better notes and, for Biology, she plans on reading ahead more.

Getting better grades is serious business for Bailey. Money is at stake. "If I don't do better this semester, I'll lose my scholarships," she says. "I've got to do better."

So far the best thing about college is the friends Bailey has made. "They're like sisters," she says. She says the worst thing so far is, of course, her grades, and also her roommates. The first roommate stole her credit card one night and used it to buy $14 worth of food at Taco Bell.

Her second roommate wasn't a good student and ended up dropping out. Currently, she doesn't have a roommate, which, as an only child, she prefers. "I'm not used to sharing a room," she says.

Her biggest conflict in college is money. Like most college students she never has enough. "I need money for books, phone bills and to help my mom out."

Her motivation comes from her family. "My mom is encouraging," she says. "My family tells me I'm great and they look up to me. They tell me I'll do good."

Bailey believes that the reason many students don't make it through their freshman year is because of partying. "Both my roommates partied and didn't go to class," she says. "I tried to wake them up for class but they slept instead of going to class. I don't party. I work weekends," she says.

Bailey's advice for new freshmen is to "stay focused on your work, on your classes. Don't let people peer-pressure you to do stuff. My friends always try to get me to go to parties. I don't go. They call me a hermit and say I'm boring, but I got my grades to worry about."

Dr. Bass

Dr. Bass is the director of the Honors Program. He also teaches Psychology and was an undergraduate at this school. I speak to him in order to get his take on what Honor students do to achieve their level of success. In other words, I want to know what makes an honor student an honor student. But I also speak to Dr. Bass because of a personal story I once heard him tell about when he was a freshman. "I was an A-B student from the North," he says, "coming to a school in the South. I thought everything southern was inferior—the cooking, the culture. I saw everyone down here as slow and backwards." He had a bad attitude. That bad attitude affected his class work and the way he presented himself.

"My first semester composition teacher pulled me aside one day," he says, "and told me I was wasting my mother's money. She said, 'You don't belong here. You're not living up to your potential. It'd be better for your family if you went home.'" Says Dr. Bass, "It floored me. She saw something in me. She did it to inspire me. I didn't get it at the time but it did motivate me. I started working hard to show her I was worthy. I earned a B in her class. I was beginning to understand my worth."

According to Dr. Bass, students in the Honors Program know they are the best. They've been told their whole lives that they're brilliant. They have confidence and as a group they feed off of each other; they spur each other on. He says that Honor students are also different from other students in that they have a certain level of intellectual skill, they respect themselves, they fought the stereotyping that was imposed on them in high school and they have learned to focus on school and not on other things.

And as students of the Honors Program, they adhere to the precepts of the program. First, they are to study two hours a day for each credit they are taking. Translation: "Study for ten hours a day," says Dr. Bass, "until you fall asleep." Second, turn off the TV, the radio, or anything that is a distraction. Just as I have students who tell me they can study while listening to music, Dr. Bass says he's had students tell him the same thing. "So we did a little experiment," he says, "to find out which was the case. Guess what—the students who listened to music while studying couldn't retain the information as well as those students who didn't listen to music."

Third, Honor students are to prepare for their classes two weeks in advance. Dr. Bass tells his students that they need to go well beyond what the professors teach and when they teach it. Students, he says, need to research what they will be learning about in future classes and bring what they learn to class. Fourth, as readers, students are to read books all summer long, and during the semester they are to read two books outside of their class work. The Honors Program is setting up a book exchange that will foster the importance of reading in these students' lives. Lastly, Dr. Bass says that Honor students are to study in groups. They are then paired off and teach each other.

Besides working with Honors freshmen, Dr. Bass teaches freshmen who are not Honor students. He says the biggest mistake he sees freshmen making is that in their search for identity they put themselves in groups that get in the way of their school work. In other words, they fall victim to peer pressure that directs them not to work hard in their classes. Other problems he sees are apathy, procrastination, and lack of self-esteem. "With males, home life problems are a distraction," he says, "and also the quest for a mate becomes too important. A problem for girls is that they want to find an upperclassman who will increase their power and status." He says that when the need for a social life becomes more important than studying, grades suffer.

Dr. Bass says that all freshmen need consistency. This means that they need someone who consistently shows concern for them, someone such as a professor or mentor. "They need someone who holds them accountable, preferably an adult," he says.

About what freshmen come to college expecting, Dr. Bass says that freshmen too often only think that college is a time to have fun. "I'm going to have a good time," he says is the prevailing attitude. "They see school as being about socialization, about having the best time of their lives. They party too much. They spend too much time with Greek life and SGA." Dr. Bass says all those things are too distracting. Somewhat surprisingly, he says that freshmen should not take part in those things at all. "They don't know what they're getting themselves into. They become too distracted and forget what they are really in school for."

For incoming freshmen Dr. Bass has this advice: "The harder you work when you get here, the easier it will be later on. You'll be prepared. Set goals for yourself, semester goals, yearly goals. Avoid distractions."

And, "If you're the smartest person in your group, you're in the wrong group."

Boring Classes

February 5

Tameka

So far the only problem Tameka has is getting up on time for her classes. She finds that when a professor doesn't close the door (which locks) on students at the beginning of the class, she has a tendency to be late. When the professor closes the door, she makes sure she's on time so she won't be locked out. As for her Critical Thinking class, Tameka says it's still hard. "I'm not a critical thinker," she says.

Tameka has yet to start at Walmart. Next week she'll start working. When I ask her if she dreads the thought of working again, she says no. "That's where most of my friends are." Tameka also tells me that she informed her boss that she'll be going home in a couple of weeks so that they shouldn't schedule her to work, when, in actuality, she isn't going home. Instead her boyfriend is coming and she wants to spend the whole weekend with him.

Curious about what Tameka does for money when not working, I ask her how she manages not working for a month. "Money is fine," she says. "My grandmother, mother and boyfriend all gave me some." Her grandmother even set up her bank account so that when she gets paid (she works for the state) a portion of the money is sent to Tameka's bank account.

Tameka informs me that her roommate has been gone for the past two weeks. Her father died. This event has meant that there has been no friction between her and her roommate as there was last semester. Having a roommate has taught Tameka though that she doesn't like to share a room. "I've never had to share a room," she says. "It's not easy."

In the past Tameka has spoken about how some of her classes were boring while others were interesting. This week I ask about what makes for a boring class versus an interesting class. Boring classes, she says, often have a professor who speaks in a monotone. She uses her Biology professor as an example. "He speaks in a monotone and never changes his tone even when he says something interesting that catches the class's attention. Like once he said, 'I grew a weed plant in college, but we're not going to talk about that.' Then why mention it?" And her Biology professor uses PowerPoint and writes on the whiteboard material that they've already read about on the Internet. "And when he talks about something, he doesn't explain it well," she says.

Tameka prefers a class where the professor asks questions of the class. She wants to be involved. "If I know the professor won't ask questions, what's the point of me paying attention?" she says. Furthermore, Tameka wants her professors to provide examples of what they're talking about. She wants to fully understand the material and not have vague discussions that are difficult to grasp. What she really has problems with is when professors are not only vague, but also tell the class "to consult a colleague" to understand the material. "What if my colleagues don't know?" she says.

There are times when part of the problem of a boring class is the subject itself. "Sometimes the topics are just boring," she says. Her examples are Biology and Critical Thinking.

On the other hand, the class Tameka finds interesting is First-Year Seminar. "I'm interested in learning about the school," she says. She also finds the professor engaging, which adds to her interest in the class.

"He comments on our papers," she says. "He talks to us about current events, about what's going on in the world and asks us what we think. For example, he asked us what we thought about benefits to poor people being cut. We had discussions on honesty and integrity, about if it's okay to cheat on a test if the professor leaves the room," Tameka says.

I ask Tameka how she would teach if she were the professor. "I would let the class teach," she says. She says she would assign each class member two pages of the textbook and have them each present to the class the information contained in those pages. I ask her what she would do if they left information out. "I'd say to them, So let's talk about what you missed," she says.

As a professor, Tameka says she probably wouldn't tell jokes to get her students' interest. "Well, maybe I might try," she says, changing her mind. "I would try to explain the material any way I can. I would do it the best way I could. I would break big words down for them. I would make up acronyms so that they would have an easier time remembering the work. I would teach everything step by step," she says. "I think I'd be a good professor."

Ashley

Usually, Ashley and I meet at three o'clock on the days I interview her. Since I'll be busy today at three, Ashley meets with me at noon. Today she doesn't look like her usual sleepy self. She seems more alert and energetic. When I interview her at three I know I am interfering with her nap time and I often feel guilty about that. Today though is different. This interview is easier than the others.

Ashley reports that her schedule now is "steady." Her English class finally has an instructor. She just wrote her first paper in that class. The topic of the paper was "Advice I would give to my high school teacher."

She dropped her Physics class. "I was a good deal behind," she says. "I registered for the class late, and by the time I got in the class they were already on chapter two." She took Physics in high school, she says, and "I didn't like it." She'll have to take Physics again or Earth Systems.

Ashley's parents will be flying down from Maryland in a couple of weeks for Parents' Weekend. They will be staying with the family friend who lives nearby. Ashley says her parents will be taking her out to eat—"I'll eat well while they're here"—and grocery shopping. I ask her if she has anything else planned for them. "They'll do what they want," she says.

With Ashley as well I ask about the differences between boring classes and interesting classes. For Ashley too, the difference begins with the professor. Ashley says that boring professors aren't "interactive." Boring professors don't talk to the class. They don't ask questions, don't act as though students' opinions matter. She uses her current English instructor as an example. "We haven't really gotten into anything interesting in that class," she says. "We come, we sit for fifty minutes, then we leave."

She also identifies boring professors as talking in a monotone. Her English instructor speaks in a monotone and so does her First-Year Seminar professor. Along with talking in a monotone, Ashley says her First-Year Seminar professor "talks a lot, more like rambling."

A very important factor for Ashley when it comes to distinguishing a boring class from an interesting class is the time it is offered. When she's sleepy she's more inclined to be bored. She has had two classes at eight o'clock in the morning—Critical Thinking last semester and Speech this semester—and even though her speech professor is "lively," Ashley is bored in that class. She says she's good from about 9:30 to 2:00. "After that it's too much," she says, as I discovered with our three o'clock interviews.

An interesting class for Ashley meets between 9:30 and 2:00 and has a professor who is "interactive." She uses her Biology professor as an example. "She is very interactive," she says. "She's ready to go. She's very energetic, uses lecture and PowerPoint. She asks questions to make sure you're paying attention. She gives examples." When talking about our prehistoric ancestors, her professor bent over and "wobbled all around the place," Ashley says.

I ask Ashley, who is an Education major and who plans to teach one day, what she will do in the classroom. "I want to be an interactive teacher," she says. "I'll use stuff like games, things that you need to know to be on top of the information," she says. Also, she says, "Since I'm a visual learner, I will use PowerPoint some."

Moreover, Ashley says, "I want to be a well-rounded teacher. I'll let students talk, have discussions. I don't like it when they sleep though. If they're sleeping, I'll give a quiz and just let them sleep. Since I'm late sometimes, I won't say anything to the late students unless they're always late." I ask about what type of voice, or tone, she'll use. She laughs. "Not this one," she says. "I won't be loud but I'll change my tone to keep students engaged. I'll ask students questions," she says. I ask her if she'll be a good teacher. "I like to think so," she says.

As she's getting up to leave, Ashley hands me a form and asks if I'll fill it out. It's a recommendation form. She says she would like to be a Resident Assistant. She hasn't heard anything about her application to be a Campus Guide, so now she's thinking about becoming an RA. I'll ask her about that topic next time.

Brittaney

Brittaney doesn't know yet what career she would like to pursue. That is why she hasn't declared a major yet. She thinks that possibly she'll end up majoring in Biology in order to work towards becoming an orthodontist (she has braces) but she just isn't sure. One thing she is sure about is that she wants to help people outside of her career. "I want to build something where I can give to the less fortunate. I'd like to start a non-profit organization." She has done volunteer work, feeding the homeless, talking to them, helping clean up the community.

Brittaney is from Detroit. Her mother is in college, majoring in Criminal Justice. She's studying to be a probation officer. Her brother dropped out of college and works on houses. Her father has been in prison for fourteen years on a murder charge. Brittaney says her father is innocent. Despite the fact that her father is in jail, Brittaney says she is close to him. "He still takes care of me," she says. "It's not like he's in jail. It's more like he's living in another state."

Brittaney says that in high school she was a "dedicated, determined student." She ranked third out of one hundred and twenty students. "I was involved in leadership activities," she says. "I was active in mentoring girls at Superfriends, For Girls Only, the Principal's club, the National Honor Society. I also took some college classes." Brittaney had a 3.7 high school G.P.A.

However, she did not do as well in her first semester of college. She received three B's—Computer Science, First-Year Seminar, Algebra—a C in English and she dropped her history class because she was receiving a D. Brittaney was a bit surprised at the grades she received. "I just knew I'd have some A's," she says. "I became very emotional because I felt like I didn't do something right." Her parents calmed her down, saying that for her first semester of college she did fine. Brittaney says that part of her problem was dealing with homesickness and "me adjusting to not having Mom pushing me to go to class." Also, she says, "I was still suffering from senioritis left over from high school."

This semester Brittaney plans on making some changes. "I'm going to the library for two hours each day even if I don't have anything to study," she says. "I'm going to go to class," she says, "even when I'm sick. I'll study harder, longer." Brittaney doesn't believe she did anything right last semester. As for what she did wrong, she says, "Everything. I have a lot of regrets from last semester. I need to be more focused and study more and take extra credit seriously."

Brittaney laughs when I ask her how much studying she did last semester. "I didn't study every day," she says. "Maybe twice a week for half an hour. I slept instead, watched TV, went out to eat."

College has changed Brittaney as a person. "It's humbled me," she says, "as far as my attitude. I had a bad attitude. I was angry as a kid because of my father's situation. I had an incident last semester where I got into an argument with a girl in my dorm. I was put on probation, had ten hours of community service added to the twenty we're supposed to do. There was a restraining order put on me."

According to Brittaney, that incident and its consequences wasn't the worst thing to happen to her last semester. The worst thing was not making it through her history class: United States, Africa and the World. She had to drop that class because of her poor performance. She says that it's a class that she's supposed to be interested in. "It's a class about my people," she says. "But history is boring. I just don't like history. Often, in my mind, I fell asleep."

The best thing that happened to Brittaney last semester was raising her mid-term grades. "I was nearly flunking everything at mid-term," she says. "I pushed myself and got better grades."

I ask Brittaney if she gets along with her roommate. "No, because I'm used to being by myself. I'm clean and organized. She's like the total opposite. And she's bossy, tells me what to do. She smokes too, marijuana, makes the room stink of it. She's a complainer as well and gets mad easily."

College is a bit different from what Brittaney thought it would be. "I thought it would be like in the movies with all the parties and having fun and something always going on, always something to do, and with lots of school spirit," she says. She didn't imagine that in college her biggest daily problem, besides her grades, would be having to purchase basic supplies for herself. "I have to buy everything," she says, "even my toothpaste and shampoo with my own money. I wasn't ready for that."

Brittany says what motivates her is her mother, the example she set as a single mother. She says that, too, she wants to be a role model for her younger brothers and for her niece. Besides that motivation, what drives her is remembering why she is here. "I must remember what I came here for," she says.

Her advice to incoming freshmen is "If you fall, get back up again."

Dexter

Dexter is a Fashion Merchandising major who wants to be a fashion and image consultant, a fashion editor for Vogue and a publicist. He's the oldest of three and is originally from Harlem. His mother dropped out of college and works for the Veterans Officers Hospital as the supervisor of the Transportation Department. Dexter is not close to his father. For the past several years Dexter has lived with his grandparents in Atlanta. To him, they are his parents.

In high school Dexter says that he was "rebellious." "I lacked motivation," he says. "I could have done a lot better. I didn't put the effort into it." His lack of effort showed in his G.P.A., which was 2.6.

Dexter also says he could have done better his first semester of college. "If I'd taken the time to study more, I would have done better," he says. "I should have visited my professors' offices during their office hours. I will do that this semester." He received an A in Art Foundation, a B in English and First-Year Seminar, a C in Science and History and an F in Algebra.

This semester Dexter says that having earlier classes will help him stay focused in his classes. Also, he says, "I will hassle my teachers for help. I will ask them what I can do to further my studies and to improve. I will ask them more questions."

While Dexter doesn't have a typical job outside of school, he says he is a "freelance wardrobe stylist and a personal assistant for a local designer." He is constantly putting information on social media for the local designer. "If you see me using my phone in class, that's what I'm doing," he tells me.

Making friends is the thing he reports as having done right last semester. "I made six really good friends," he says. "We all have the same major." What he could have done better is become more active on campus. "I wasn't very involved," he says.

According to Dexter the worst thing to happen to him last semester was his grades. "I couldn't believe I failed a class. I never failed before in school." Dexter says that last semester he didn't study every day. "I studied four hours every other day." He is learning how to be more focused now on academics. He says, "I've matured a little since high school. There I was always in drama. College has given me an outlook on the real world. Life moves fast. I gotta live each moment to the fullest."

The best thing that happened to Dexter last semester, he says, "is being on my own, not having to ask for help, growing up and becoming more mature. Something else that was beneficial to him last semester was rooming with his RA, who was a graduate student. "We got along," he says, except for the fact that his roommate wasn't as neat as Dexter.

Dexter says the best thing about college is becoming "geared toward your career goals and meeting people like professors who can help you get to where you want to be." He says the worst thing is "being broke, begging parents for money and eating Ramen noodles."

Along with being broke, Dexter says that for him his biggest daily conflict is the fierce competition he has with the other fashion majors.

"We're all aspiring for the same thing," he says. "You have to learn to take criticism and talk to people. There's a lot of butting of heads. Not everyone agrees on the same fashion."

Dexter's motivation comes from his grandparents. "They inspire me to do many things," he says. "They gave me freedom to do and to be whatever I want without judging me."

His advice for incoming freshmen is "not to let anyone get in your way of what you aspire to be. Go after your dreams."

Dr. Foster-Singletary

Dr. Foster-Singletary has taught composition and literature at two HBCU's and is herself the product of an HBCU. She says that she attended a high school in South Carolina that was mostly white. She felt "isolated" in high school, "devalued" and "vulnerable." She chose to attend an HBCU because she wanted "not to be the only person of color in the class. I wanted to be validated, my interests and things I thought important validated."

For a decade Dr. Foster-Singletary has been helping her students see their worth and validating their abilities and interests. Along the way, she has made many observations about her students, especially freshmen. From what she has seen in the classroom, freshmen don't often make it beyond their freshman year because they "lack a clear sense of what they should be doing in college, what their experience should be like. They lack focus." She says that often students are too interested in their social life, or, as she says,"in making babies."

Another reason she says freshmen have difficulty their freshman year is "a lack of support from home." She says that besides students not understanding what they should be doing, sometimes students' families don't understand either. "I had a promising student in my one class," she says. "She was the oldest of several and they kept calling her to give them money and to fix problems at home. She felt guilty and let that guilt interfere with her schoolwork. Eventually she left school and went back home."

Dr. Foster-Singletary says that students, who are the first in their family to go to college and who don't have the support from home they need, have a difficult time recovering from problems that might arise or from distractions that they let come between them and their schoolwork. "They don't have the human resources to recover," she says. Dr. Foster-Singletary stresses that to be successful in the classroom students need to be focused on their schoolwork and they need to be consistent. "A focused student comes to class, sits in the front row, doesn't hide from the professor, asks questions, does all the work and comes to the professor's office," she says. "A professor wants to see the student focused on the class and consistent in her performance. If you're consistently a student who the professor sees working hard then more than likely that professor will give you some slack if something unforeseen happens that affects your work," she says. Consistent students "set themselves up to recover when they face illness, make mistakes, or have family issues."

For example, "My freshman year I had a migraine for a couple of days that knocked me to the floor. I was too sick to go to class or write a paper that was due. Somehow I got myself off the bed to write the paper and turn it in. When my professor handed it back to me, she said, 'I don't know what this stuff is but I'm giving it back to you.' I got an F on the paper." She hadn't realized that she should have spoken to the professor beforehand about what was happening, but since she was a consistent student, her failure on the paper "didn't tank the whole semester" since she "had been doing good work."

I ask Dr. Foster-Singletary what expectations freshmen have that they shouldn't have. "They expect you to hold their hand," she says. "There's too much of that—they say they don't know where to print their papers, they don't have a stapler, or they'll say something like 'I couldn't find any books on my topic.'" She also says that their expectations concerning their "workload aren't realistic. They don't understand the college-level workload."

Dr. Foster-Singletary has three pieces of advice for incoming freshmen. The first is "your schoolwork should occupy the majority of your time and energy." The second: "You'll have to work harder than you think you do." Finally, "Hang around with like-minded people."

Beneficial Classes

February 17

Tameka

Tameka is worried these days. She's worried about her Critical Thinking class, she's worried about French and she's worried because she's having trouble sleeping at night. Students who've had her Critical Thinking professor have told her that "the class starts out easy and then slams you with tests and many people fail." She's seriously thinking of dropping the class. In French the professor is "moving so fast" that Tameka doesn't feel as though she can keep up. "I'm used to Spanish," she says. "I had Spanish in high school. I'm stressing out over this."

Part of Tameka's problem is that she hasn't started yet at Walmart. "I'm not used to not working," she says. "When I'm working there's no time to worry. Right now I'm just waiting, waiting, waiting for Walmart to call me back. I don't think they're going to call me till March." Her worrying has affected her sleep. And last week it snowed, which forced the cancellation of classes for three days, giving Tameka more time to worry. "I didn't do schoolwork," she says. "I watched TV, ate. I feel bad now." Instead of sleeping at night she took naps that lasted up to three hours. To overcome some of her worries, Tameka says that she's going to talk to her Critical Thinking professor. Maybe talking to him will give her the peace of mind she needs to sleep at night.

If there's any good news for Tameka it's that she and her roommate are getting along better. Tameka attributes the change to the death of her roommate's father. "Since her father died, she's not so bad," she says. "If she had the same attitude she has now we probably wouldn't have gotten into it," Tameka says.

Tameka also tells me that she has signed up to be an RA for next year and that she has two grades to report, 85 on a Pre-Calculus test and 97 on a Critical Thinking quiz. "That's good, isn't it?" I say. "A 97 on the class you're afraid you're going to flunk?" She shakes her head. "It was a take-home quiz," she says, "and the answers were in the back of the book. I should've gotten a 100."

Curious as to whether she learned anything valuable from her classes so far in college, I ask what sticks in her mind from last semester's classes. From her history class she says she learned the importance of following directions and writing well. "My professor for that class was a lawyer. He stressed the importance of writing well." From her Speech professor she learned the importance of saying thank you. "My Speech professor said that students ask her to write letters of recommendation but they never say thank you," Tameka says. "She taught us that a thank you goes a long way." When I ask if she's been fascinated by anything she's learned in her classes, she says, no, she hasn't.

Tameka says that her most beneficial class is First-Year Seminar because her professor teaches "life lessons." Recently, her professor posed the question to the class, When you're old and look back on your life, what will you say your purpose on Earth was? To make the class ponder their purpose on Earth, he had the students write their obituary after their having died at the age of seventy. Here is part Tameka's obituary:

"Tameka was an ambitious and family-oriented woman. She was a very hardworking and caring person, always helping and giving back to the community. Over her lifetime Tameka did many wonderful things. She is most recognized for her scholarship foundation 'Nothing Is

Impossible' and her charity event 'Give, Give, Give.' She also was recognized for treating patients that could not afford dental treatment; she would even go out of the country every year to treat foreigners as well. She lived by the quote, 'If you put your mind to it, you can do it!'"

Ashley

Ashley spent the snow break last week with her roommate at the family friend's house nearby. She says she "relaxed and ate better food" while there. "I wanted to do my schoolwork," she says, "but I didn't get much done." In fact Ashley says that in general she hasn't been studying these days. She did receive some grades since we last spoke. She got 93 on the paper in English on which she wrote to a former high school English teacher to explain what lessons her teacher should share with students to prepare them for college. "I said my teacher needs to teach students about responsibility, time management and dressing right," Ashley says.

She also got two A's on speeches she gave in Speech. In her first speech, she introduced herself. She receive 100 but was told to "avoid space fillers such as um and to watch hand movements and pacing." The other assignment was an impromptu speech about the one place she would like to travel. "I said Italy because I'm a pizza fanatic and they have more authentic food there," she says.

I ask Ashley why she wants to be an RA. "Because of my RA's," she says. "The RA on the second floor of my building helped me get acclimated to the school and gave me advice on things in my field. I want to help people like that. I want to help them transition from high school to college. I want to help students like I was helped."

As with Tameka, I ask Ashley what—if anything—she learned from her classes last semester that she finds valuable. She says that in her history class she learned that "if you don't understand something, you have to speak up and ask. I don't really care about history so it's not easy for me to catch everything the professor says. I learned I have to communicate when I don't follow so that the professor doesn't hurry over the information and I miss it." From Critical Thinking she learned how important sleep is. The class met at eight in the morning, and, when not getting enough sleep, Ashley learned she had a hard time getting through the class. She figures it was important for her professor to get enough sleep as well to get through the class. "Like us I'm sure my professor wanted to be sleeping," Ashley says, "but it was like we all just got to stay up and get through this together."

I ask her if she was fascinated by anything she learned. It takes her a while to respond. When she does, this is what she comes up with: "I'm fascinated how often people who don't come to class and still pass." I ask her how she knows they passed. "I think they passed," she says. "I like to think the best of everyone."

This semester Ashley says the valuable thing she is learning is how to overcome her nervousness in front of people and deliver a speech. "I can't look at other students," she says. "Everyone's looking at me so I look at the clock and move my eyes from the clock to the corner of the ceiling then back to the clock."

About this semester thus far, Ashley says, "I've been chilling these days. The snow days helped me catch up on my sleep."

Sean

Sean, from Queens, New York, is a Mass Media major who would one day like to work on Enews and "do something for Ralph Lauren," such as be a host for his fashion shows. Sean is from a family in which, he says, "everybody went to college except for my father." His father is a Verizon technician, while his mother "works behind the desk for the fire department."

In the Catholic school Sean attended, he was the "popular guy who got his work done but who got in trouble at the same time, usually for talking too much." One of his teachers called him "the life of the party." Sean says about attending Catholic school, "I liked it. I always knew what I was going to wear and there were always things going on at school." Sean achieved a 3.3 G.P.A. in high school.

He expected to do the same in college. "I thought I'd do a lot better than what I actually did do," he says. He received four C's—in English, Math, Speech and First-Year Seminar—a B in Science and an A in Sociology. Part of the reason for his low grades was that, he says, "I focused on classes I wasn't doing well in and neglected the others." Sean also admits to studying very little. "I studied two hours on Saturday and two hours on Sunday and I'd study right before a test."

Sean says that if he did anything right last semester it was not putting off his homework. "I did my homework when it was due," he says. Also, getting a math tutor was something he did right. What he did wrong, he says, "was studying for the classes I thought I knew instead of studying for the classes I didn't know." This semester he says that he's going to study harder, "not slack off in class and I'll actually pay attention more."

College has changed Sean as a person in that "I'm learning the value of a dollar," he says. "Mom didn't send me to school this semester with as much money as she did last semester. Last semester, I blew right through my money in two months. I ate out a lot, went grocery shopping. This semester I'll eat more in the caf"—he doesn't like the food in the caf—"and not go to so many parties."

The first month of college didn't go very well for Sean. First he had strep throat, then tonsillitis and finally pink eye. Being sick was easily the worst thing that happened to him his first semester. Even though he was sick he still went to classes and joined campus organizations. He joined the Tri-state Club, the Radio Club, the Pre-alumni Club and the Broadcast Club. His uncle warned him that these organizations were taking time away from his studies, but Sean wasn't so sure. He did, however, quit the Broadcast Club.

Sean says the thing he likes the best about college is "the freedom." "I have the freedom to choose my class schedule, to go places. I set my own limits." What he likes least "is the line in Financial Aid and also their attitude. There's a man who works there with a bad attitude."

College isn't different from what he thought it would be. "I knew what I was getting myself into," he says. He knew about college from his family and "from common sense," he says.

Sean's biggest conflict in college is a tad different from your average college student. His biggest daily conflict is that there is "no yogurt 24/7" in the cafeteria. They just have it in the morning. On a more serious note, when he was sick early last semester, he says his biggest conflict was that the clinic wasn't open on the weekends, and, he says, "It closes early on the weekdays. I really needed it last semester when I was sick."

Sean is motivated by "the amount of zeroes on my future bank account and the smiles of people who invested in me." What's going to get him through his freshman year, he says, is "keeping in contact with people back home and making sure not to be bored. When I'm bored I do bad things," he says.

According to Sean the reason some freshmen don't make it through their freshman year is that they "get too lazy, too comfortable, too distracted. They're too worried about parties and boyfriends and girlfriends. They need people watching over them, checking on them. The village needs to follow them," he says.

Sean's advice for incoming freshmen is to "come in with an open mind but not an open heart. Don't be ready to tell someone your deepest, darkest secret. Have them tell you first."

Also, Sean says, "Be ready to see weird fashion."

Jasmyn

Jasmyn is a Fashion Design major from San Diego who would one day like to create her own evening gown and business suit line. She is an only child. Both of her parents went to college. Her mother is a probation officer who also teaches psychology at the University of Phoenix. Jasmyn is not close to her father and is unsure what he does for a living.

She earned a 3.5 G.P.A. in high school and was, as she says, "very busy." She was a member of the Dance team, the Poetry Club, the Speech and Debate Team and was involved with Theatre Arts. Jasmyn says that her high school was harder than college. Her first semester grades were not, however, as good as her high school grades. She earned a B in English, Math, Sociology, a C in Biology and an F in Art. "I had trouble my first semester managing my freedom and free time," she says. "I put things off. That's why I didn't do as well as I thought I would."

Ending her proclivity for procrastination is one of her goals this semester. "I need to stop procrastinating," she says. "I got to stop pushing things back." Another thing she says she needs to do is ask more questions. "I can't just think I know what's going on or that I'll catch it later," she says. "I have to ask my professors questions so I know what's going on in class." Also, Jasmyn says she'll change how much she'll study. Last semester she studied only thirty minutes to an hour each day. "I only worked on the subject that had some type of homework," she says. "I will change that. And I'm going to write my papers early and have you look at them"—since I'm her English professor—"and have tutorials with my science professor."

College has brought Jasmyn out of her shell. Part of the reason for that is her roommate. "We just clicked on move-in day," she says. "We stay up late talking to each other," she says. In fact they stay up until two or three in the morning even though they have eight o'clock classes.

They both try to find time later in the day to take a nap. Jasmyn and her roommate also go to parties together and do each other's hair. "We have hair nights," she says. Besides these activities with her roommate, Jasmyn is an ambassador to the athletic department, attending all home games for the sports teams. She also helps out coaches and shows recruits around the campus.

The worst thing that happened to her last semester was when her roommate started having seizures at a party and they spent the night at the hospital. A less serious problem for Jasmyn was her lateness. "Twice I woke up late for the same class," she says. "I hate that. I'm never late!"

What Jasmyn likes best about college is that even though "I make mistakes, I have room to grow here. I'm with people who are trying to figure it all out," she says. "We're trying to figure it out together."

For the most part college is what Jasmyn thought it would be. Her mother talked to her about college, preparing her for life on a college campus. I ask if her mother gave her any advice. "She told me to stay out of trouble and don't go to jail," she says.

Two things motivate Jasmyn. The first is "the fact that school costs so much!" The second is her dream to become a fashion designer. "Ever since I was nine and I saw *That's so Raven* on TV my dream was to become a fashion designer," she says.

The thing she is going to do to make it through her freshman year "is to stay focused. I will be with people who have the same mindset," she says.

Her advice to incoming freshmen is that "you don't have to do it all, not every event, not every party. Your education is more important than everything else." Finally, she says that incoming freshmen need to "breathe."

Dr. Taylor

Dr. Taylor has taught at an HBCU for thirty years and also graduated from an HBCU. She teaches Sociology and is from Virginia. She was raised by parents who didn't graduate from high school. She says she went to an HBCU because "that's what I was familiar with. That's where my relatives and peers went."

For thirty years, Dr. Taylor has seen students come and go, and she's made some observations in that time. She says that students in the past had more of a sense of why they were in college and what it was they wanted to get out of it. They had more of an "eagerness and enthusiasm" to learn. Today's students, she says, "feel more sense of entitlement." Their mindset is "if I'm here I'm entitled to a good grade and to graduate. Their sense of learning is not as great." She is quick to say that this difference in today's students is not exactly the students' fault. "You can't just point the finger at the students," she says. "Sometimes part of the blame can go to the school and the professors."

There are certain behaviors students sometimes exhibit that Dr. Taylor says interfere with their learning. "There's too much focus on what students see other students doing," she says. "They see their friends aren't studying so they don't study. There's peer pressure. Students who want to study think there's something wrong with them if they're not hanging out with friends." As for distracting behaviors in the classroom, Dr. Taylor doesn't lock the door on late students or have a "no phones" policy. She says that she tells her students that they shouldn't be late to class, that college students are expected to be on time and not come late and disrupt the class. As for phones and tablets, she says that many times they are using those devises for the readings in the class, so their usage is fine in the classroom, unless it's obvious those devises are being used for another purpose. Recently, she saw a female student in her class texting. Dr. Taylor said to her, "We don't do that in here." "I didn't want to hurt her feelings," she says. "So I took her aside after class and told her what I expected from her and that I was sure she could succeed in my class."

From what she has seen over the years, Dr. Taylor says that high-achieving students come to class, "make an attempt to engage with the class, do the assignments, ask questions and do the extra credit even when they don't need to." She further says that high-achieving students not only read the supplemental readings for the course but they ask for more to read. Moreover, these are the students who get a "glimmer" in their eyes during class, as if to say, "Oh, I want to get this, to know more about this."

To become a good student, Dr. Taylor believes that besides coming to class, students should "always study their notes against the class readings, and they need to find a peer partner—a study buddy they can rely on." She also says that to be a good student you should never be afraid to ask for help from your professor, and you "should never be caught wondering what's going on. Seek out a reliable person who can help." And good students, she says, "Should be involved in the campus activities that will further their education."

If there is anything that prevents students from becoming good students, it is lack of "confidence." "Many students have been in schools where their potential has not been fully developed. HBCU's nurture students and help them to believe in themselves, help them to explore opportunities." On top of gaining confidence, she says that students need to look at school as they would a job. They need to be consistent—come to class, do assignments on time, study for tests. College, just like a job, is a commitment students make and which they need to dedicate themselves to, says Dr. Taylor. "You don't skip a day of work just because you don't feel like working." School should be approached the same way.

Dr. Taylor's main piece of advice for incoming freshmen is to "attach yourself to professors who serve as your role models." She says that when she was in college that is exactly what she did. "I tried to follow them and do what they did. They gave me advice, which made my time in school much easier." Dr. Taylor says that she learned that "teachers enjoyed students who put their best out." Students who gain the professors' respect are the students who grow and do well, she says.

HBCU's vs. PWI's

March 3

Tameka

After a three-month hiatus, Tameka is back at Walmart. She just worked her first day. "I got to get used to working again," she says. They have her scheduled for thirty hours this week, but first they have her take CBL's again, which she describes as computer training and warning after warning about joining a union. Tameka says one time a union representative came in the store and tried to hand her a leaflet. "We were told never to sign anything from unions or take what they try to hand you," she says. She didn't take the leaflet.

Tameka is feeling less stress as far as her studies are concerned. She met with her Critical Thinking professor and he assured her that she understands the "basic parts" of what he is teaching. He told her not to give up. She didn't drop the class and received a 98 on the latest quiz. She did however drop French. She's going back to Spanish, a language she had in high school and one she figures will be beneficial to her when she becomes a dentist.

Other grades to report are an 82 on the first Biology test and a 59 on a history test. About the 82 in Biology, she says last semester she flunked the first Biology test, so, needless to say, she feels pretty good about her 82. Concerning her F in history, Tameka says, "I need to learn her teaching style first. I need to study the right things. The page numbers in our book are different from the ones in her book. I'll be better prepared for the test we're having tomorrow."

For Valentine's Day Tameka's boyfriend sent her a bouquet of flowers. This past weekend he came down with his mother, got a room with a kitchen and made Tameka a home-cooked meal. They exchanged gifts as they celebrated a late Valentine's Day in person. She got him a pair of jeans, while he got her two Pandora charms for her charm bracelet, two shirts, socks, candy, three teddy bears, a Valentine's pillow, and a stuffed monkey. "That's a lot of stuff!" I say. "He can give me more," Tameka replies.

For Spring break, which is next week, Tameka says she's staying here and working at Walmart. She also plans to make study guides for Critical Thinking, First-Year Seminar and to complete an extra-credit assignment in history to help her grade.

This week I ask about thoughts she has on HBCU's. First I ask how HBCU's are different from other schools. She says, "Fried chicken Wednesdays—they probably don't have that at other schools." Also, she says, "They have smaller classes than big predominantly white schools [PWI's]. And dorm visitation rules." She means the strict dorm policies that are imposed on our students here, that family and friends can't visit the students' rooms. "If my cousin wants to come down here and spend the weekend with me, she can't," Tameka says.

I ask her if anything would be different if she attended a PWI. "Maybe less stress about how I'm going to pay for next year," she says. "I don't know what kind of help I'm going to get. I haven't looked into it yet."

The best things about attending an HBCU? "Being able to meet with your professors one on one, the long withdrawal period and fried chicken Wednesday. But not fried fish Friday!"

Ashley

Last week Ashley's parents came for Parents Weekend. She says that Friday her parents did "stuff on campus." On Saturday and Sunday they went to breakfast with her, took her grocery shopping, to the Cheesecake Factory and cooked at the house of a friend who lives nearby. I ask her if her parents had a good time. Ashley shrugs.

If there's any complication to Ashley's semester so far it's her English class. At the beginning of the semester the class didn't have an instructor because it was a newly-opened section. For two classes the class received no instruction. Recently, the professor who had been teaching the class got sick and needed to be hospitalized and isn't returning. For a week Ashley says they didn't have a professor. A new one has been assigned but Ashley doesn't know what grade she was receiving from the original professor. "I don't know what's going on in that class," she says.

In her Biology class Ashley received the same grade Tameka did on her first test—82. I ask her what she thinks of this grade. "Eh," she says, making a face. "I guess it's good. She told us the class average was 64, but I want all A's."

For Spring break, Ashley says that she and her roommate are taking a bus home. They bought the tickets for $55 apiece. They wanted plane tickets but they waited too long to buy them. The drive on the bus will take them about thirteen hours, she says.

When it comes to HBCUs, Ashley says from what she's seen there is less school spirit. She thinks the reason is that HBCUs are small schools with lackluster sports teams. Also about HBCUs, she says, "Our food is worse."

Ashley says that if she attended a PWI she would probably have more diverse friends. In her high school, which she estimates was fifty percent white and fifty percent black, she had white and black friends. She enjoyed having friends of both races. She says, "My white friends would think of the weirdest stuff to do and it would become fun."

At first Ashley doesn't know what to say when I ask her about the best things about attending an HBCU. I ask her if it's learning about African American history, as so many students have told me over the years. "Just open a book," she says, "to learn about African American history." Then I tell her that I've had many students tell me that they came to an HBCU to be surrounded by other black people like themselves. "You don't learn more positive things about African Americans because you hang out with eighteen and nineteen year olds," she says. "You're learning about your generation and why you don't like them. Sometimes it's just black people complaining about why they don't like black people."

Eventually, Ashley mentions the best thing about attending an HBCU. "It's fun. You meet people, become friends, make memories. African Americans like to socialize and here there is a high volume of socializing." She says that she likes the way rival HBCU's stick up for each other. "Even if they don't like each other," she says, "they stick up for each other against outsiders."

Ashley says the downside to HBCU's is that all black people are seen as needing to go to an HBCU. "We're expected to go," she says. "If you don't go, black people think you like white people more."

Amy

When Amy came to school last semester the university mistakenly listed her as a Mass Media Arts major. She had the school change that listing to her intended major, Business of Sports Management. But soon after, she decided that she wanted to be a Psychology major, so she changed once again. On second thought, she realized that maybe the school had been right to list her as a Mass Media Arts major, so she changed back to her original major. All of this took place in Amy's first semester.

Amy is as unsure of her major as a freshman can be. She is just as unsure about her career goals. She says, "I want to do something with entertainment, or I want to be a fixer for companies. If something goes wrong, I want to fix it for them. My backup plan is law school. I want to be a defendant lawyer. I want to work with abused kids, like a family lawyer."

An only child from Virginia, Amy comes from a family with a college-educated mother who is an accountant and a father who was in the navy and is now a manager at Babies "R" Us. As a high school student, Amy says she was "really lazy." "I didn't apply myself. I didn't take school seriously until I started to apply to colleges. I would have been a good student if I'd applied myself. Her high school G.P.A. was 2.7, and she ranked 305 out of 503 students.

In college Amy figured she'd receive A's and B's, and, then, in return, her good grades would qualify her for a scholarship. Unfortunately, her first semester grades did not qualify her for a scholarship. She received one A, three B's and two C's. "I was disappointed in my math grade [B] and my First-Year Seminar grade [C]," she says. "But I'm proud of myself when I compare my grades to what other students got. For doing little work I did pretty well. I know I'll get better grades in the future."

Amy will make some changes this semester. "I'll make sure I go to classes," she says. "Last semester I didn't get up sometimes to go to classes. I'm not a morning person." Her earliest class last semester was a 9:00 class that met Tuesdays and Thursdays. Other changes she is making include learning to balance her social life with academics and keeping a planner to organize her days. She'd also like to study better than she does. "I don't know how to study," she says. "I can't focus. I don't retain information when I read." Amy says that she listens to music when studying because "I need sound when I study. Otherwise I fall to sleep." Last semester, Amy estimates that she studied about two and a half hours a night. She says that for tests she began studying two days prior to test day. To study for tests she used "flashcards, writing things down and I tried to read the textbooks."

As for the things that she did right, Amy says turning in her homework was the thing she did right in the classroom. Outside the classroom, she managed her money well and built an excellent relationship with her roommate, who, like her, is an only child. "We have a good connection," she says about her roommate. "It feels like we've known each other for years."

Amy says, "Wow," when I ask her how college has changed her as a person. "It's made me more independent," she says. "Also, I'm more accepting of other people. Certain things people do irk me, but I don't let it bother me. I'm more comfortable around other people and more comfortable with myself."

The worst thing that happened to Amy last semester was having her phone stolen. The ironic thing about having her phone stolen is that Amy was coming back from court after being sentenced for evading a fair on the train. "I was out of money," she says, "and some guy said I could sneak in on his card, but the security guard was right there and saw me." A judge sentenced her to twenty hours of community service. After the sentencing, a guy followed her as she got off the train and snatched her phone from her hand and ran off. Amy says her community service consisted of office work such as filing. She also had to pick up trash outside.

Having her cell phone stolen might have been the worst single incident that happened to her last semester, but the ongoing tension with one of her suitemates proved a major headache for Amy. "She's the complete opposite of me," she says about her troublesome suitemate. "She's messy, loud, selfish. We had fights over cleaning the bathroom and her being loud on her side of the suite. We yelled at each other, RAs got involved. We almost had a fight." This semester, Amy says, "We just don't talk to each other."

What Amy likes best about being a college student is the independence. She says that she's "still trying to find" herself and that college gives her that opportunity. What she's had a hard time getting used to in college is being surrounded by "so many people, waiting in line in the cafeteria and having so many rules" to live by. I ask her what she thinks of the food in the cafeteria. "It's not as bad as students make it out," she says. "They have their good days and bad days" in the cafeteria.

College is different from what Amy thought it would be. "On TV those college students don't seem to have any rules. They can do whatever they want," she says. Another difference is that there isn't much to do that doesn't cost money, and none of the surrounding businesses offer student discounts. Amy says that her mother didn't tell her much about college but her aunts did. "But they were talking about when they were in college," she says. They told her that there were a lot of free parties, but Amy says that most parties cost between $5 and $20. "They also told me that when you're in college you get care packages from home all the time. Mine have been few and far between," she says. Considering her college experience, Amy says, "College is fine. I just get homesick a lot."

Amy says that what motivates her is "making sure I can give my parents what they gave me. I want to make sure they're well off, that they live a comfortable life. I want to buy my mom the clothes she wants and I want to buy my dad the car he wants—an Audi."

The reason many college students don't make it through their freshman year, Amy says, "is because partying is a real big thing. They don't know how to balance partying and studying." Also, she says, "Some don't know that they're not meant for college. Not everyone is."

Amy's advice for incoming freshmen: "It's okay not to know what you want to do."

Amy also says, "Everything your parents told you kicks in when you're in college."

Jim

Jim is a Fashion Merchandising major from Macon, GA. His goal is to work with high-end fashion, working with runway models and with celebrities. He is the first in his family to attend college. Jim says that his father recently went on disability, and his mother "just doesn't work."

In high school Jim says he was an "overachiever." "I was the president of Future Business Leaders of America, secretary of the Beta Club, on the school news, a member of the Ambassador Club, started the first fashion show called Project Recycle, I was the junior class president and the Homecoming King." He graduated fourth out of fifty-nine and had a 3.5 G.P.A.

Jim was pleased with his first semester grades in college. "Except for English, I did better than what I thought I would," he says. Jim received an A in Art, Math, Biology and Sociology. He received a B in English and First-Year Seminar.

Because of his good grades Jim says that he doesn't plan to do anything different this semester. "I'm still going to cram," he says. "Cramming works best for me. I don't know how to study. I don't retain information. I forget it by the next time I go to class," he says. Jim also says that he makes sure only to party on the weekends. "I set weeknights aside for school," he says. Also, he says that he wasn't too active on campus and instead "focused on my G.P.A." Jim says that school is too expensive not to focus on grades.

One thing he says he could have handled better last semester was an altercation with his roommate. "We were about to fight," he says. They had an argument that carried over for several days and got progressively worse. "I'm scared of the dark," Jim says, "and my roommate unscrewed all ten of the light bulbs and took them out. I started screaming and yelling and ran out of the room. I texted him that I paid for five of those light bulbs and he better put them back." His roommate did. This semester Jim has a different roommate, and they get along well. The only problem he has is with his suitemates. "No one ever wants to clean the bathroom," he says.

College has made Jim less selfish. "There are so many people everywhere and you're forced to interact with them. I've learned I can't always get my way."

The best thing that happened to Jim last semester was "getting financially enrolled. I didn't get financially enrolled until two weeks before the beginning of the semester," he says. "I needed to get six thousand dollars." The best thing about being a college student is "the freedom. College is just like high school but with more freedom."

What Jim dislikes about college are the cliques. "We have so much freedom and places to be but people don't interact outside of the cliques," he says.

His biggest daily conflict is getting dressed. "I don't always feel like getting dressed. I just want to wear jogging pants to class." Jim says that fashion designers like dressing other people but not themselves. "We get tired of clothes," he says, "and don't like to dress."

When I ask Jim what motivates him, he says, "I don't want to work a job. My granddad told me if I don't want to work I should go to school. That way I can at least do something I want to do."

Jim's advice to incoming freshmen is to "Work, work, work, then play later."

A Model Student

I first encountered Jeanine several years ago in a 300-level British Literature class I was teaching. She was one of those students who always came to class, was always on time and who spoke when I asked questions. She never had her phone out or used it in class. The first papers she wrote, while not A papers, showed promise. What impressed me the most about her was the drive she showed to become a better writer. She wasn't one of those students who asks me, "How do I get an A in this class?" as if there is a secret formula for getting an A. But rather she was one of those rare students who would come to my office a week before a paper was due and have me look at her rough draft. A day or two later she would have me look at another draft that incorporated the changes I had suggested. By the end of the semester Jeanine was turning in A papers. My thought was, I hope to see her again in other classes of mine. Fortunately, she took four more. In each class I became more and more impressed with her.

Jeanine was born in the Bronx and raised in a single-parent home in East Harlem. Her mother, a high school dropout who worked for child care services, moved Jeanine and her twin brother seven times in their childhood. "We moved because of money or the area," Jeanine says. "At one point four of us lived in a studio apartment."

Despite their living conditions and despite the fact that Jeanine often attended schools that she says were full of "out of control kids," her mother stressed the importance of education. "My mother made sure we were on time to school," she says. "After school each day she asked us what we learned, made us read every night for thirty minutes and she checked that we did our homework. She signed it in the upper right corner to show our teacher that she had checked it. My mother told us how important school was."

Jeanine says that in school she was "always the star student. I was always the one student who cooperated with the teacher, but I didn't like to be the center of attention. I didn't want to be seen as showing off." One year in middle school, Jeanine's teacher took her aside and said, "You are a breath of fresh air. I wish everyone could be like you." Because of her serious approach to her education, for as long as she has been in school, Jeanine has been called by her classmates "the teacher's pet." This label has even followed her to college. "Twice here other students have called me the teacher's pet," she says. I can hear it in her voice that she is bothered by the name calling; however, she knows that she is the one who has her priorities straight and that the name callers do not.

Describing herself as "independent, self-disciplined, hard on myself, focused and curious," Jeanine had all A's in high school except in her math and sciences classes, where she usually had high B's. She took several AP classes and college-prep classes and attended a college program that met twice a week, which covered such topics as preparing for the SAT and applying to college.

To pay for college Jeanine has loans from the government and she also has private loans. She has a merit-based scholarship from the school, an AmeriCorps scholarship and this year, because she is an RA, she has an RA scholarship. Her financial house in order, her mind focused on school, Jeanine did well her freshman year. She received a 3.7 G.P.A. The only class she struggled in was Pre-Calculus. "I got my first ever C," she says, frowning and shaking her head. "I've always struggled in math." Jeanine says that in picking her major she knew it would have to be one that had something to do with writing. "I knew I just had to write," she says. She narrowed her choices down to Communication, Journalism and English. She chose English.

The key to her success her freshman year was her study habits. "I was locked in my room four hours every night," she says. "All I did was study. I got my work done ahead of time." She says that her practice is to begin studying for tests two weeks ahead of time, and, for papers, she begins the preliminary work on them three weeks prior to their due date. I ask her if now, as a senior, she studies more each day than she did as a freshman. "Yes," she says. "Now I put in about five hours a night." Her current G.P.A. is 3.62.

Concerning her social life during her freshman year, Jeanine says, "My main focus was school. I was alone most of my freshman year. I partied when I needed to, when I needed relief, usually about two or three times a month." She did have a group of friends, but she says, "I had a different mindset from them. They smoked pot, drank, went out every weekend, hung out at night. I didn't do that stuff. I would attend poetry readings. They didn't want to do that." Also, her freshman year Jeanine served as the historian for her residence hall, taking pictures of events and keeping a timeline for the hall.

Since her freshman year, Jeanine has served as the sophomore president of Kollege Kids Incorporated, which is a talent-based organization; as a member of Young, Fit and Fly, a mentoring organization; as a member of the English Club; as an RA; as a mentor at a preparatory school. She has also worked in the library, has had two paid internships, and she is president of the English Honors Society, Sigma Tau Delta.

Her plan for after graduation is to work for Teach for America. After that she would like to work in library archives and/or pursue a Master's in Library Science. Eventually, she wants to go back to New York and work in the archives of the Schomburg Research Center for African

Americans. She worked there during her junior year of high school, partaking in group activities. She says about her time at the Schomburg, "That's where I learned the majority of my black history. I want to go there and give something back." Jeanine adds that she would also like to work for the Smithsonian Museum.

I ask her about advice she has for new freshmen, as it is my belief that they would be wise to listen to someone of Jeanine's caliber. She says, "Know your goals. Know why you're in school—for your education. Everything else can wait. Put off socializing, manage your time wisely, build strong relationships with your professors and network with the right people, such as your professors and internship leaders."

Spring Break/First Tattoo

March 24

Tameka

A half hour before our appointment, Tameka sends me a text. "Good morning [,] I have a toothache and I barely wanna open my mouth [.] [I]s there another time we can meet?"

We agree to meet two days later at nine in the morning. She doesn't arrive. Later she texts me, "I am just wakin [sic] up[.] [T]his week has not been my week[.] I missed class too."

A day later I text her to email me what's been going on. She doesn't reply.

A week later, she texts the following: "Worked 38 hrs [,] caught a cold and had a toothache then my wisdom tooth start[ed] growing in grrrr [,] missed class Monday and one class wed. No fried chicken wed. [,] got a 96 on bio test, 92 on bio lab test [,] 78 on history exam [,] no critical thinking exam yet."

She also sent a picture of her midterm grades. She has three B's, Biology, History and Pre-calculus. Two A's, Critical Thinking and First-Year Seminar.

Michael

Here is an email I received from Michael:

"Hello, Dr. DeLong

Of course it's me [,] Michael. I can give you a run down on my life. So much has [gone] on from December 15th [. . .] . Wait[,] first I decided to join the South Carolina Army National Guard. My ship out date was January 15th [. . .] but of course things [don't] always go as planned. When I got home (Columbia SC) I found out that my parents are separated. With them being separated I had to make a decision which parent I wanted to stay with, so I decided to stay with my mother. I figured it would be ok staying with my mother because it would be close to my job. So I work and worked and worked. I work at this pizza place called Bellacinos. Like I said I was supposed to ship out January 15th and finish basic and AIT training all by May[.] I was going to take summer classes at Midlands Technical College here in Columbia South Carolina but I still haven't left for basic yet. During my road to enlisting into the army I had many complications. When I went to MEPS (Military Enlistment Processing) they checked our weight[,] height[,] blood pressure, drug tested, HIV/AIDS test, everything. I had to gain 13 pounds but I only gained 7. First time I went to meps my blood pressure was extremely high which temporarily disqualified me. That pushed my ship out date back as well. I had to go to my doctor for blood pressure readings for 2 days and send my records back in. It took the doctor about 3 weeks to approve it because it was during those snow days and the doctor was out. On February 22, the doctor approved my medical record but my ASVAB (test to get into the military) scores expired. So I had to take the test back over which I scored 20 points higher. After all I enlisted into the National Guard on March 12 and I ship out to basic on April 1st (no april fools) I will be stationed at Ft. Benning[,] Georgia. I graduate basic on June 12th and on June 17th I fly to Ft. Lee Virginia for AIT training where I learn the job I chose which is a 92Y Unit Supply specialist. I graduate there on August 12th and I'll be moving in back [to school] on August 16th. That pretty much sums up my life within the past couple of months."

Ashley

Today Ashley wears a sweater with a wide collar, exposing much of her collarbone. I notice what looks like a tattoo. I ask her if it's new. "Yeah, I just got it last week," she says. "It's the word *strength* with the infinity sign." I ask why she chose that word. "You have to stay strong," she says. "You can't let stuff get to you. Stuff happens. When there's a bad day, a good day follows." I ask if her parents know about it since it's her first tattoo. "Mom saw it, but Dad doesn't know yet. Mom said she wished I didn't get it but that she respects my decision. You know what," she says to me, "I appreciate that. Mom also says she hopes I don't get any where people can see them."

Ashley says that during Spring break, which she went home for, she "caught up on my sleep, did some homework, went out with friends." She says that mostly she was "doing nothing." When she came back she got her midterm grades. She received all A's except in Calculus where her grade was 89.5. Her professor told her she doesn't round up midterm grades.

About her English class she says, "I don't know about that class. It is peculiar in nature." That's the class that was late in receiving an instructor, then the instructor had to leave because of illness and a new one took over several weeks ago. She says that the class wrote one paper for the previous instructor but she doesn't know if this instructor is using that grade. The new instructor did give them a pass/fail midterm and she guesses that's how he determined what midterm grade to give each student. Ashley says about her new instructor, "He talks about what we're going to do, like these first ten thesis statements—he's been talking about them for weeks. While he talks I either listen to music, get on Netflix, snap chat. We don't do anything. If I didn't go to class I'd still pass that class."

In her Speech class she received a 92 on an informative speech she gave on HIV AIDS. She gave background on the disease and explained how HIV AIDS affects people in Africa and in the U.S. Ashley lost points for going over time and for saying um and for hand gestures that she wasn't aware she was doing when giving her speech. I ask if she spoke on the topic because it is meaningful to her. "Yeah, I mean I guess," she says.

Ashely interviewed for an RA position. She interviewed with the head of Residence Life and other officials. She says it went well. She was asked why she wants to be an RA and if she could be a vegetable, which one would she be? To the first question, she answered that RA's are influential in helping young women make the transition from high school to college and RA's can teach how a young woman should act. To the second question, Ashley said the vegetable she would be is broccoli. "I said broccoli because it's diverse—you can eat it raw, eat it with cheese sauce, in Chinese food, in salad and it still tastes good. Some people eat it on their pizza, but that's weird." I laugh. "That's what they did too," she says. "They laughed too."

Also, Ashley had to do a desk duty shift with an RA. She sat at the desk with an RA in another building than hers and got to see what that was like. "I got to see how they set up for events," she says. "It made me excited." I ask her about having to enforce rules that she might not agree with, such as the rule that parents and relatives aren't allowed to enter dorm rooms. "I have to think of it as my job," she says. "It's a job that comes with benefits. I must enforce the rules. I have to think that if I bend the rules for one person then more will want special treatment, then you have chaos." She says that if she became an RA she wouldn't want to lose her position; therefore, she will enforce the rules.

The last thing she did as part of the interview process was what's called "Behind Closed Doors." Ashley says, "They give you scenarios and you act as an RA. Two guys started a fight and I had to handle the situation. They said I did good." For the second scenario they had her sitting at the desk and "a mom tried to go in the hall." For both scenarios Ashley tried to talk to the participants and when that didn't work she "called" public safety. The important thing she was told was that no matter what, RA's shouldn't touch anyone. I ask if that is for liability problems, but Ashley says she doesn't know.

This week I ask Ashley about a topic nearly all students have to learn about as freshmen—financial aid. Ashley says that financial aid wasn't completely foreign to her. In her high school, the counselor explained financial aid to them in her junior year. And when she arrived at college, her mom handled her financial aid discussion. Ashley says, "I just sat back. It wasn't new to my mom. This was her third time" (because of her brothers). Ashley says that when it comes to the financial aid from the school what she took away is that "[t]he school is stingy. If you don't ask for it, they're not going to give it."

Reggie

Reggie emails me. Here is what he writes:

"I don't like my new school that much because it is in the country and it's very boring. My roommate is from Houston and he is Nigerian and isn't very clean. I like to stay to myself here and I don't talk to a lot of people. I visited my friends back at [our school] last week for spring break and that was cool. My midterm grades are pretty good. I have A's in Art, College Comp. II and Algebra and a B in Communication Applications. I miss [our school] and can't wait to come back. I go home to Dallas a lot since I'm closer to home. I think I covered everything [. . .]."

Jamie

Jamie chose English as her major because she wants to be a writer. "Ever since I read Toni Morrison's *The Bluest Eye* I wanted to be a writer," she says. "My dream is to be a famous writer and teach creative writing. Besides writing, Jamie is a saxophonist on a band scholarship who is inspired by Kenny G.

A Chicago native, Jamie says that her mother went to college for two years and that her uncle graduated from college. Jamie is an only child whose father is "not in my life." Her mother is a stockbroker.

The four words Jamie uses to describe herself as a high school student are "lazy," "smart," "popular" and "procrastinator." She graduated with a 3.1 G.P.A., which is pretty much what she expected her first-semester G.P.A. in college to be. "I thought I'd make the honor roll. I would've been okay with a 3.2 or 3.1, even a 3.0," she says. Instead she received a 2.4 her first semester. In part, Jamie believes the problem might be having band practice five days a week from 5:45 to 9:30. In high school her band practices were only an hour long. Also, she attributes her low grades to partying. Besides parties on the weekend, she also went to some weekday parties. What she has learned from last semester is that she has "to work around" her band practice schedule and she can't party as much.

Although she didn't study enough last semester, Jamie says there were some things she did right. "I went to class for the most part, did my homework," she says. "I wrote poems, I exercised (rode the bike, treadmill, lifted), and I stopped myself from fighting someone." She had an altercation with a girl in her building who "had an attitude and was loud and in my face." Jamie says, "She was kind of attacking me. I didn't want to hurt her. I didn't want to get kicked out. I didn't fight and I'm still here."

Jamie says that her studying last semester consisted of studying for only fifteen minutes a day ("if that") and not studying every day. "I studied thirty minutes to an hour before a test," she says. "That didn't work out well."

Besides her grades, the worst thing that happened to Jamie last semester happened one day during band practice. "I got caught chewing gum," she says. "I forgot I was chewing it. I had to stand in front of everyone, stick my gum on my forehead and do push ups. Then I had to do 'smurf jacks.' That's a jumping jack at the level of a smurf, bent over." I ask what's wrong with chewing gum at band practice. "Gum destroys instruments," she says, "and it's disrespectful."

The best thing to happen to Jamie was that "I got with my girlfriend. She's my roommate." What she struggles with is "being so far from home." She says she Skypes and Facetimes with her mom often. She also has what she describes as her "circle of friends" here. She started with six friends but because of disagreements and miscommunication the circle is down to four.

Jamie cites band as her biggest daily conflict. It takes up much of her free time. "I feel like I could do so much more with my writing if I had time," she says. "I could get a job or an internship. Band gets in the way of all that."

What motivates you? "The fact that I want to be a writer. I can see a little girl picking up a book of mine and feeling the way I felt when I read *The Bluest Eye.*"

Jamie's advice for incoming freshmen concerns partying. She says: "Limit the partying. Study, go to class and pay attention. Don't go to class with a hangover."

Aja

Aja is from San Francisco. She's a Social Work major who wants to work with children either at a children's hospital or with a group home through a foster care agency. She wasn't a foster child herself but she "moved around." When her father was sent to jail, Aja and her two sisters moved in with her grandparents. Neither her mother nor her father will tell Aja why her father is in jail. Despite this difficult situation, she is still close to her father. "We talk on the phone all the time," she says.

Aja is the first person in her family to attend college. Her mother is a high school graduate who works in human resources at a company. Not until her junior year in high school did Aja decide that she wanted to go to college. Before then she says, "I didn't really care at all about school. I did the minimum to pass. I pulled it together in my junior and senior years." She increased her 2.7 G.P.A. to 2.9. "I was happy that I improved my G.P.A.," she says, "but sad I didn't get it up to 3.0."

She did much better her first semester of college. She received a 3.5 GPA. Most nights she tried to get in three hours of studying, but, she admits, that she didn't study hard every night and that is something she wants to improve on this semester. When she wasn't studying, she was "sitting on Instagram."

Last semester the things she did right include balancing her studying with her partying and making good grades. Also, she says, "I've done what's best for me. I learned to put me first. For example, at home I would do what my friends do; here I don't. I don't want to smoke and I might not want to drink. I'm turning away from peer pressure."

Aja credits college with helping her grow up "a lot." "I've learned not to depend on my mom for everything. We're very close. My mom is my 'partner' and we lean on each other." Besides growing up in college, Aja says she has learned a good "work ethic." She says, "I work hard—college sets my life. This is where my career begins."

The worst thing that happened to Aja last semester was "leaving my mom." They flew to school together and her mother stayed for ten days at an aunt's house. "Watching my mom cry on that last day was horrible," Aja says. "I cried when I went back to my room. For a month after that we talked on the phone four times a day."

The best thing that happened last semester was "making the friends that I did." Also, she had her first "real" relationship with a male. "Things didn't work out," she says, "but I learned from it."

This semester Aja has a new roommate. Last semester, however, Aja had a roommate she describes as having "poor hygiene habits." She didn't clean, do laundry and she didn't shower. Aja and some of the other girls on the hall tried to tell her roommate about her smell, but her roommate had a hard time with what they were telling her. "Do I stink!" she said. "No one else is telling me this, only you guys." Aja says the smell was so bad that even when her roommate wasn't in the room the smell was still there. On top of that, her roommate would talk on the phone loudly late at night when Aja was trying to get enough sleep before getting up for her eight o'clock class.

Aja says that what she likes the best about college is the freedom and independence. "I feel like an adult that doesn't have to pay bills," she says. "I like the parties too, especially the free ones." What she likes least is "being so far from my family. If I could just move them here, there would be no cons," she says.

Her biggest challenge is getting enough sleep. She says that on Mondays, Wednesdays and Fridays she usually gets to bed at around 12:30, but on Tuesdays and Thursdays she doesn't get to bed until two or three in the morning. She stays up those nights talking to friends or watching something on Netflix. I ask her if she takes naps. "All day, every day," she says.

What motivates Aja is "wanting better than my mom could give me. I want to give my kids what my mom gave me and more. And I want to help other people." She also says, "I want my degree from a black college. I like it here so much."

Aja's advice to incoming freshmen is to "get scholarships." She says, "Financial aid is not free money—you will have to pay it back!"

Financial Aid

Most students who attend college will, at some point, have to visit the financial aid office. Upperclassmen have learned about financial aid and how the financial aid office functions; for most freshmen, however, financial aid and the financial aid office are a mystery. When freshmen are in the dark about funding for their education, problems, and sometimes, heartbreak occur. To get a better understanding of financial aid and what freshmen need to be aware of, I spoke to Mr. Missouri, a senior advisor in the Office of Student Financial Aid at my school.

Mr. Missouri says that students should look at paying for their college education as if they are buying their first house. He says they both cost about the same, especially if the student is attending a private college, and money borrowed to pay for it will need to be paid back to whomever the student borrowed it from. Often, Mr. Missouri says, students have no idea how much their education is going to cost and their parents either don't know or they don't tell their child. "Too often students and parents think if they can make it to school, then it's the school's responsibility to see to it that the tuition is paid," he says. "Nothing about paying your tuition is magical," he says. "It is a bill. If you can't cover the bill, then this isn't a reality for you."

He gives the example of a male student from Detroit, who drove to school with his mother. "I couldn't break through to them," Mr. Missouri says. "His charges, where the aid was coming from. His mother said to me, 'I found a way to get him here. You need to find a way to get him through.' She said that since the school had more money than she did, she expected the school to pay for her son's education."

Students need to know what everything will cost. And, he says, they need to read the papers they sign. "Students usually don't read anything they're signing. When they find out what's in the documents they signed, they feel slighted. They need someone to blame. They don't want to take responsibility." He says that students need to be responsible and understand that they are the ones who will owe the money, not someone else.

I ask Mr. Missouri what the top three misconceptions are that freshmen have about financial aid.

"It's easy, automatic, readily available, an entitlement. Students think, this is my money, it belongs to me."

"That it is inexhaustible. They don't realize there are caps. You can only borrow so much."

"Applying and paying it back is someone else's responsibility. Helicopter parents are crippling kids—the child doesn't read what he's signing and expects his parents to take responsibility like they do with everything else. But this is a contract with the student, not their parents."

Mr. Missouri says that the typical college student, especially one who is first in *Spongebob Squarepants* his family to go to college, is in the dark about financing his college education. "About seventy percent or higher don't know anything about financial aid," he says. For example, he says, students usually don't know that financial aid is a loan from the United States Government. Students aren't getting information about financial aid in high school either usually because counselors are swamped with all the other things they have to do. "The vast majority of students come on a wing and a prayer," he says. "They don't understand anything about getting financial aid."

I ask him what gets students the angriest. He says, "When they are accepted and don't have what they need financially. It's demoralizing for the student and for the school. Lots of students end up crying. There's a lot of crying in this office. All that work they did to get accepted and now we're telling them they aren't financially enrolled. This might be the first time they've been given a solid no in their lives." When this happens, Mr. Missouri says to them that they should have had a savings plan; they should have had some type of plan before they arrived at the school.

Mr. Missouri has three pieces of advice for students who plan to go to college.

"Know your story—when you file for financial aid you have to know who your biological parents are. You need to know where the money is in your family. This information affects how much aid you can get."

"Students need to speak to parents about financial matters. They must ask them how much money they make. They need to talk to their parents about starting a 529 or an Education IRA."

"Students need to find people who will fight for them because students need people who will support them in any way. They need to look everywhere they possibly can for help. One student I know has eighteen scholarships. Eighteen! She hustled everywhere she could. Students need to look to their families, churches, and other organizations they belong to for support. They need to use social media to raise money. Sites like Kickstarter are a good place to start." Lastly, Mr. Missouri says that students should study the financial aspect of their education the way they would study for a test in a class.

"I Don't Do Trash"

April 7

Tameka

Tameka tells me about the dental problems that caused her to miss our meeting last time. "I was biting down on something in the back of my mouth and it knocked out part of my filling," she says. In the same area, one of her wisdom teeth has started to come in. Since then she's been taking medicine that numbs that side of her mouth. But sometimes the medicine wears off when she's sleeping and the "throbbing pain" wakes her up. She says that she'll wait until she goes home after the semester to have her teeth taken care of.

At first the pain of her dental problems was so bad that it forced her to miss two classes on separate days. She missed her Biology class on Monday and her math class on Wednesday. In her Biology class, Tameka reports that they are dissecting a pig. Says Tameka, "I'm the note-taker. I'm not touching that pig." And in her history class, Tameka's professor lost the results of two quizzes the class took back in January. "They were two, thirty-question quizzes we took online," she says. "She sent us an email beating around the bush about what she was going to do. She says she's working on fixing the problem but that we have to take those quizzes again. She told us, 'If you passed it the first time you should pass it the second time,'" Tameka says about her professor. I ask if this is a problem for her. Tameka says, "I had a hundred on those quizzes. I don't want to take them again!"

Because of the problems with her teeth, her professor's losing her quiz grades and her difficult work schedule, Tameka is going through a rough spell. She is scheduled to work a thirty-eight-hour workweek, which starts at two and ends at eleven at night. "I don't get to bed till two," she says. "But I can't fall asleep." She's been relying on naps. "When I get back from class I take a nap," she says. I ask her how she's fitting in studying. "It's fitting," she says.

Like Ashley, Tameka has also applied to be an RA and has gone through the interviewing process. At her interview they asked her, first, if she could be a candy bar, which one would she be, and, second, if she could be a bike part, which one would she be? "For the candy bar I said I'd be a Snickers bar," she says. "Because who doesn't like a Snickers bar? For the bike part, I said the handle bars. I need to control where I'm going."

A very interesting thing happened to Tameka during the "Behind Closed Doors" part of her interview. "Behind Closed Doors" provides scripted scenarios and the prospective RA must respond by demonstrating what she would do to take care of a situation. Before she entered the building, Tameka noticed four campus patrol cars in front of the building and assumed that the officers were part of the activities she was about to participate in. In her scenario two guys started fighting in front of her. Tameka called for public safety on her phone and immediately officers came in and put handcuffs on the two males. "I assumed the police knew I was acting," Tameka says. "I thought they were part of the act."

It turns out they weren't part of the act. They took the two males out to the squad car and put them inside. "I thought they were playing with us," Tameka says. The two males thought the same thing. The police, however, weren't acting, and when they found out it was all an act, they got angry at Tameka for calling them. The woman running "Behind

Closed Doors" had to calm the police down. "The officer apologized and gave me a banana," says Tameka. "I didn't eat it. I threw it away." Since then Tameka has not heard from Residence Life concerning her candidacy to be an RA.

The last time we spoke, Tameka mentioned her worries about paying next year's tuition. I ask her about it. She says she saw someone in Financial Aid but that she still isn't sure how she'll be able to pay. "They better give me a scholarship," she says. And if they don't? "I don't know. I haven't thought about that yet. I don't want to take out another twenty-thousand-dollar loan," she says. "You'd have to do that every year?" I ask. She nods. "I could buy a nice car every year with that money," she says, "or a semi-decent house."

A few days after we speak, Tameka sends me a picture of her grade on her Critical Thinking test. She received a 91. This is an important grade for her because there are only two tests in the class, this test and the final. After all her recent difficulties this test result must feel good.

Ashley

Today Ashley looks the way she did when we used to meet at three in the afternoon: tired. "I need a nap," she says. She's been in classes since eight o'clock and is ready to head back to her room.

I ask about what's going on in that English class of hers. "I didn't think we had class today," she says. "I got there on time but he wasn't there, so I went to get breakfast." She came back twenty minutes later and the instructor was there. "We don't do anything in that class," she says. They haven't written any papers yet. "We started a literary analysis, but we didn't do that. Now we're doing something else." She says it again, "We don't do anything in that class."

Things are going well for Ashley in Calculus, where she received an A on a test. It's a different story in Biology. "I got a 68 on an open book test," she says. "I didn't study for it." She had been getting an A in that class, but now it's a B. If she can get her grade back up to an A she won't have to take the final, and of course she would prefer not to take the final. In Speech she'll be giving a persuasive speech on the same topic of her informative speech, AIDS. When I ask her what she will say, she says, "I have no idea."

There is no word yet on whether she was chosen to be an RA.

I haven't asked Ashley about her roommate in a while. I ask if having her best friend as her roommate prevents her from making other close friends. "No, I still have close friends," she says. "I can't prevent her from having close friends either. We're two very mature people." She says they don't have these types of problems.

There is one persistent problem they do have that Ashley mentioned to me last semester—she hates to take the trash out. She rarely ever takes it out. "I don't do trash," she says. "Back home my brothers did it. But I did it the other day because they were checking our rooms and I wanted to avoid getting a fine. My roommate said, 'Oh, look, she's taking out the trash.'"

A smaller source of conflict is the TV shows they watch. They have one TV in the room. It's Ashley's. They watch many of the same shows, but Ashley also likes to watch some cartoons, such as *SpongeBob Squarepants*. "My roommate calls them stupid shows," Ashley says. "At first that bothered me. I'm like how do you know if you never watch them?" Otherwise they don't argue over the TV.

Ashley is contemplating a change these days. She's thinking of changing her major from Education to Math. She still plans on becoming a teacher, but she's heard it's a better idea to get her degree in a specific subject, then get her teaching certificate later. She is mulling this over.

Renae

Renae's goal is to become "a family and couple's therapist." "I'm a person who gives advice," she says. "My friends tell me I'd make a good psychologist." She's an only child from Atlanta, whose mother is an accountant and whose father is deceased.

"As a high school student, I was mediocre," she says. "I did mediocre work. I didn't push myself. I was more interested in socializing." Renae had a 2.7 G.P.A. in high school. In her first semester of college her grades weren't much better. She received two B's, two C's and an F in math. "I felt horrible," she says. "I could have done so much better. I didn't study enough. Math has always been a problem with me. I should've gotten a tutor."

Renae says that getting that F last semester was the worst thing to happen to her. She tried to hide her grades from her mom. Her mom found out about the F anyway. "She wasn't mad," she says. "She just told me I should've worked harder." This semester she says she is studying more. "Last semester I really didn't study," she says, "maybe thirty minutes a night."

What she says she did right last semester was "staying to myself." She says she "didn't get into a mess. I learned to take myself out of situations." Two of her suitemates didn't get along and often had words but Renae remained neutral and didn't get involved. "I kept my distance from both," she says.

Outside of the classroom Renae is a busy freshman. She and a friend have started a club called Embrace. They speak at the Boys and Girls Clubs. They address the girls, talking to them about beauty. "We try to uplift the girls," she says. "We talk about self-worth, self-image, self-respect." Renae says that girls are insecure about the way they look. She teaches that girls must "love their flaws." With her mother, Renae helps the homeless by giving them food bags and blankets. She would like to intern with a local feed the hungry program.

Things didn't start off too well with her roommate last semester. "I tried to avoid her," she says, "because of what my suitemates told me about her." But then one night they talked for a couple hours and Renae discovered that her roommate wasn't anything like she'd been told. "Now we're close," she says.

Besides her roommate, what Renae likes best about being a college student is that she is now thinking for herself and taking responsibility. What she doesn't like are the rules she has to live under in the dorms. She doesn't like the limited hours that friends can visit, that family can't come into her room and that only students from neighboring colleges can visit.

Renae says that because of things her mom told her she had something of a sense of what college would be like. "Mom said college would be hard, that I'd need to stay focused. She said college wasn't fun." However, Renae got a different impression from TV shows such as *A Different World* and *Boy Meets World.* She wanted to believe that TV shows were providing an accurate portrayal of college life. What she learned was that both her mom and the shows were accurate up to a point, and that neither prepared her for her biggest daily conflict—waking up for classes. Renae has a habit of staying up until five in the morning—"I can't go to sleep early"—which makes waking up for early classes quite difficult.

From her observations, Renae says that the reason some freshmen don't make it through their freshman year is because "they forget the reason they came here." She also says that sometimes networking is stressed over education and students begin to see their job as getting to know people over studying.

To make sure she keeps her focus on her education and what's important to her Renae believes in helping others, and "keeping positive people around me, people that uplift me and who are working hard to get where they need to be."

Renae's advice for incoming freshmen is to "stay focused—college is more than having fun. You need to study, study, study! This is not a game."

AG

AG learned to love little children through a Vo-Tech program at her school, where she was given the opportunity to watch children in a day care. Because of this love of children she came to college as an Early Education major but switched her major to Business with a concentration in Marketing and Entrepreneurship when she realized she also loved marketing. Her career goal is to combine her two loves by owning a day care business and franchising it.

Both of AG's parents graduated from college and she has an older brother who currently attends college. AG is from Memphis, Tennessee, where her mother is a private nurse and her father is a training manager for Honey-Baked Ham. AG describes herself as a "laid-back" high school student who didn't party or even go to the prom. Due to taking weighted classes such as AP Trigonometry, History, English and Pre-Calculus, AG received a 4.7 G.P.A. in high school.

The lone non-A grade she received her first semester in college came in Biology. She received a C in the class. "My teacher was foreign," AG says. "She was hard to understand. I missed two assignments at the beginning of the semester because I hadn't bought the software yet and I got behind."

This semester AG says that what she has done differently is to make sure not to sign up for eight o'clock classes. She is also going to the library more. Also, she says, "I'm telling people 'no' if they ask to hang out or do something. I have to study more." Last semester she studied two hours a night. This semester she's studying three to four hours a night. AG would also like to be more active on campus. Last semester she didn't become involved in any campus activities.

When I ask her what she did right last semester, she laughs and says, "I didn't drop out." Then she gets more serious. "I stayed true to myself. I didn't change. I went to class every day. I made sure my grades were good." As for what she could have done better, AG talks about how she wasn't prepared for some things she saw. "I wasn't prepared for real-life scenarios," she says. "At the clubs they would be fighting right in front of us. I wasn't ready for things like that."

AG's freshman year has been a challenging one for her. On top of studying for classes and worrying about her grades, she has had the added challenge of family problems interfering with her life. Last semester, her parents announced that they were divorcing. AG's eleven-year old sister was so devastated by the news that she attempted suicide. Her sister is better now, but that event and her sister's well-being weigh heavily on AG's mind.

Her parents' divorce and its aftermath was easily the worst thing that happened to AG last semester. The best thing was learning about herself and the importance of the lessons her parents taught her. "I came to understand why my parents taught me the things they taught," she says. She explains that when she was younger she got in "trouble a lot for not doing my chores. My parents took my phone away from me and wouldn't let me go out. Now when I go out I'm conscious of what I see and do. My parents prepared me for that. I thought they were just being mean," she says. She's learned that she's growing into the person her parents wanted her to be.

This semester AG doesn't have a roommate. Last semester she says she got along with her roommate until one day they got into an argument through texting about the bathroom. "I honestly can't remember what the problem was," she says. "I told her that we'd talk about it when I got back to the room. When I did get back she was all packed up. She moved out. She left." This event left AG baffled.

Like nearly all college students, AG says the thing she likes the best about college is "the freedom." Unlike most college students, she says that one of the best things for her is "keeping up my grades." In college she has to push herself, which is something she enjoys. She further cites living in the city as one of the best things about college, but she also says it's one of her least favorite things. "The other night a bum with a shopping cart sang outside my window at three in the morning," she says. "I thought, okay, this is the city."

AG's family is constantly on her mind. She says her family's problems are her biggest conflict in college. She says, "I have a hard time focusing on school while stuff is going on back home." Yet it is her family back home that she says motivates her. "I want to give back to them. They always gave to me so I want to give something back to them."

AG says that the reason some students don't make it through their freshman year is that they "lack support." She also says, "They need someone on them, helping them. And sometimes they have problems that arise. I didn't know the problems that I was going to have."

There are three things that AG says are helping her get through her freshman year. The first is "staying on top of my work. I plan on keeping my grades up." The second is "thinking in advance. I must plan what I want from my next three years." The third is "applying for scholarships." AG plans on cutting down the portion of her tuition that she must pay.

AG's advice for incoming students is "Don't forget yourself. Don't forget your morals. Don't become a different person. Be true to yourself."

Freshman Awards

April 21

Tameka

When I ask Tameka how she's doing she tells me that she's been working thirty-eight to forty hours these past weeks. "Because of Easter," she says. "We're very busy. And people are getting ready to move out of the dorm rooms. They're buying totes, cleaning items."

Tameka is also busy with her school work. The semester is nearly over. The last time we spoke she was upset that her history professor was making her class take two quizzes that they'd already taken. Once again, Tameka got a 100 on each of them. This week she's concerned about her Critical Thinking class. While she's happy with the A she got on the test, she's worried that she's not understanding syllogisms. "It's confusing," she says. "I was reading the book this morning. The author's telling jokes and saying a lot of other things. Just give me what I need to know to get me through this."

In Biology she says her chance of finishing with an A is fifty, fifty. She has a B in the class right now and the final only counts for ten percent of her grade, so she has her fingers crossed.

What frustrates Tameka this week is not being invited to the Freshman Awards. She expected to be invited and to win an award for having a 4.0 G.P.A. When she asked why she wasn't invited, she was told that she's considered a transfer student since she transferred credits from the community college at home. "But I was a high school student when I got those credits," she says. "That shouldn't count against me. I don't understand this." Tameka worries that being considered a transfer student will affect her scholarship. Also, she feels as though she's been robbed of something she worked hard to achieve, and, therefore, deserves. Of all the things we talk about today, it is clear that this is what bothers her the most.

At the beginning of the semester Tameka said that she was going to join the Pre-professional Health Society. I ask if she did. "Nope," she says. "I never took the time to get in contact with anyone. Once I went back to Walmart . . . ." I ask too about the Biology Club, of which she is a member. "They had one meeting, but I had to work."

Any word on becoming an RA? She says that there was a meeting for all the prospective RAs. "They said they would send out a test on the rules and regulations but they didn't," she says. Tameka estimates that there were about seventy students at the meeting and that there might be about forty openings. In other words, there is a better than fair chance she'll become an RA.

Becoming an RA would help her with her financial situation for next year, which she hasn't spent too much time thinking about since we last spoke. All she can say is, "Hopefully I get a scholarship. How I'll get it, I don't know." She's applied for two, one from the Virginia Credit Union and one from the Great Lakes Scholarship, which is where she gets her Parents-plus loan. Each scholarship is for $2,500. Her plan is to apply for three more, the Buick Achievers Scholarship and "whatever I find on UNCF," (United Negro College Fund).

Tameka says that she knows someone with lower grades than her who received a $10,000 scholarship from the school. She is baffled by this. "I'm a better student," she says. "How did she get that scholarship but not me?" I ask about her finances—how much has she saved? She says she has $2,000 currently saved but that "I could've saved more. I spent

$3,000 on Christmas. I wanted my family to have a good Christmas. My mom doesn't have a lot of money."

Thinking I'm changing the subject to a happier one, I ask about her roommate. Last week Tameka brought her roommate to my office and they seemed quite comfortable with each other. I assume things are going well between them. "We're not on good terms," Tameka says. "I came in late from work the other night talking to a suitemate. Right away she says to me, 'Can you please be quiet! I don't have time to deal with that tonight.' I said, 'Whoa, you crossed a line. You don't have a job. I should be the one complaining.'" Her roommate said to her, "You don't know how loud you are." Since the death of her roommate's father, Tameka had been giving her roommate the benefit of the doubt, but this episode broke her. "I told her I won't be rooming with her again," says Tameka. Since she said that, "[i]t hasn't been peaches and cream" between them.

I ask Tameka if she has a favorite class this semester. Her answer is a simple "No." She says that she still doesn't like Biology, even though it's her major. "I don't like the professor. He's the same one I had last semester. He's boring. And I have him next semester for Microbiology!"

Least favorite class? She says they're all contenders. "Critical Thinking is my best/worst class," she says. "I came in knowing nothing. I've learned a lot from that class, and the fact that I can get a 91 on a test makes it the best class. It showed me I can do it." All the worrying she does over that class makes it the worst.

I ask her if she has any worries about her collegiate future. "Not getting a 4.0 this semester," she says. "That's the only thing I'm worried about." She says she worries more about that than how she's going to pay for next semester.

Ashley

Ashley's English class is still the strangest thing about her semester. I ask if she has any grades yet in that class. "I don't even know," she says. "We're supposed to be writing two papers in three weeks but he hasn't told us when they're due. He says he has a goal when he wants them." I tell Ashley that when I walked by her class I saw her staring at her phone. "I was on Instagram, Twitter and I was texting," she says. "He talks the whole time, all fifty minutes. We haven't done a thing in that class." Later I ask if that class has been her least favorite this semester. "Yes," she says. "I'm not learning to better my writing." She says she doesn't mind going to her other classes, but she minds going to her English class, yet she goes.

Do you have a favorite class this semester? "Not really," she says. "I just go to class." Her Calculus class meets three days a week; two of the days the class is an hour and fifteen minutes, the third day is fifty minutes. She says the day it meets for fifty minutes isn't so bad. About her speech class, she says she doesn't mind going, except that "it's just early" (eight o'clock). On her persuasive speech about AIDS she received a 93. "I spoke on getting tested and knowing your status," she says. She was downgraded for "talking too fast." She says that overall she feels more confident now when giving speeches and that she makes better eye contact than she used to.

Ashley is not a fan of her First-Year Seminar class. "We don't do anything in that class," she says. She doesn't mind her Biology class because "[m]y Biology professor is funny."

Unlike Tameka, Ashley received her invitation to attend the Freshman Awards. I ask her if she's going. "They told us we have to," she says. Do you expect to win anything? "I don't know what the categories are. I have no idea," she says.

Last time we spoke Ashley was considering changing her major from Education to Math. This week she says she probably will make that change. I ask what math classes she'll have to take if she changes. "Calc. one, two, three, Linear Algebra, Analytical Geometry," she says. About advanced math, she says, "I don't know why I'm good at it. I just get it." I ask if she could teach it since she's thinking now that she might become a high school math teacher. "I like to think I'm good at explaining it," she says.

At the beginning of the semester Ashley said she was thinking of joining the Women's Leadership Council. I ask if she did. "No, I didn't find any information out about it," she says. "Who'd you ask?" I say. "Nobody," she says.

I ask if anyone else in her family found out about her tattoo. "Yes," she says. "They all know. My grandmother called it a bug and my father told me he was going to scrape it off with a Brillo pad." I ask if he was joking or if he was serious. "He was joking and serious," she says. Regardless, she says, "I may get another one."

James

A senior from Milwaukee, Wisconsin, James changed his major twice. "My parents wanted me to be a Biology major so that I'd make some money but I changed it to Education because I discovered I loved working with kids when I worked for a non-profit for teens," he says. He wanted to major in Secondary Education, but the school only had a primary education major so he changed his major to English with the thought that he would get his teaching certificate after he graduated.

James laughs when I ask him what his plans are after he graduates. First he says, "I don't know." Then he tells me that a preparatory school has offered him a teaching position and that our school has also offered him a position in one of the offices. "But I want to travel," he says. "I've been thinking of getting a job with Carnival Cruise Line. They have a position where you work with the kids on board," he says.

Turning his attention to his freshman year, I ask James what his perceptions of college were when he came here as a freshman. "Everyone made it seem really hard," he says. "I expected to work. I knew that you had to learn to balance fun with work." At first, having too much fun was not the problem. Not having a job his first semester was the issue. "Without a job I had so much time to procrastinate," he says. "I put my schoolwork off and got a 2.2 G.P.A. my first semester." His second semester he got a job. This forced him to get his schoolwork done, which helped him achieve a 3.2 G.P.A. his second semester. Another reason James cites for not doing so well his first semester was getting involved in a relationship with an older person who didn't live on campus. This caused him not to be as involved with his schoolwork and the campus as he would have liked.

As a freshman, James says that his biggest challenge was "being in a setting with mostly black people." The high school he attended was quite diverse, being made up of Latinos, whites and blacks. "I was used to having a diverse group of friends," he says. He says that here, at an HBCU, everyone seemed the same at first. Attending an HBCU became less of a challenge when he learned to "look at the differences in the people." He remained close to his friends from high school and they're what helped him get through his freshman year, especially through his bouts of homesickness. "We vented over the phone," he says. "We cried together to get over our homesickness."

I ask James in what way(s) was his freshman year his easiest year and in what way(s) was it his hardest? It was his easiest because of the excitement he felt being in college. "Everything was new to me," he says. His freshman year was his most difficult year because, he says, "you have to make so many adjustments." You're finding yourself, learning to be away from home. It's hard when you don't have someone to fall back on. I had to do everything on my own—coming here, financial aid, etc. My parents didn't help with those things."

When it comes to his first year in school, James says the thing that he'll remember is his shock at the food in the cafeteria. "It was weird," he says. "I wasn't used to southern cooking. They were serving fish and grits for dinner. I was like, What is this? I'll always remember that."

About being a college student in general, James says the thing he likes the best is talking to the school students he works with at the prep school where he's an aide. "They look up to me because I'm a college student," he says. "They're so eager to get to college and to talk to me about it. It makes me want to work harder." What he'll miss about being a college student are his friends and his professors. "I'm so nervous now that graduation is so close," he says. "Graduating will be like leaving home again, like leaving my family again. We'll be going our separate ways."

What he won't miss about college is "waiting on financial aid. I also won't miss final exams," he says. "But there is more I will miss than I won't."

Advice he has for incoming freshmen: "Find those people to surround yourself with who will be with you until your senior year, people you can lean on for help; find a mentor on campus. It could be someone older like a professor."

Also, James says, "Don't close yourself off from any experience. Open yourself up to things you haven't done before, to those things that you say, Oh, I'll never do that—that's the thing you need to attempt."

Kristine

Kristine is a Speech Communication major from Richmond, VA. She started out as a Print Journalism major because she loves writing. Then she became a Radio, TV, Film major because she thought she wanted to be on TV. Then she realized that wasn't what she wanted to do, so she became a Public Relations major, but came to the conclusion that that wasn't the major for her because "I'm not the person everyone comes to." She spoke to a professor who gave her the advice to major in Speech Communication.

Writing is her first love and she would like to write novels. But as for what she will do once she graduates, she isn't sure. "Internship, magazine or newspaper editing?" she says. "I don't like school, but I'm thinking about graduate school. The jobs I'm looking at say you need a Master's."

When Kristine first came to college she perceived college as being fun, as a place to meet new people and as a place "to expand my knowledge." She also saw college as "a place to come out of my comfort zone." Kristine describes herself as an "only child who doesn't like to party." She says that her first semester of college she didn't have any fun. She didn't do well, having received an F, a D, a C and a B. "My mother threatened me," she says. Her mother said, "If you don't get better grades, I won't take out any more loans for you and you'll have to come back home and get a job."

Her second semester of her freshman year she did much better, making the Dean's List. However, she also had a problem with severe depression for which she did not seek help. The depression impacted her grades thereafter. Her current G.P.A. is 2.9. Only recently has she gotten help. "My depression prevented me from doing better," she says. "I was in denial about it, drinking and doing drugs. I didn't take medicine. Instead I tried to self-medicate, which is what my friends told me to do. But that wasn't what I needed," she says.

Kristine says she had other problems that prevented her from doing better. "Time management was a big problem for me," she says. "I didn't use my time to study, not at all." Instead she got involved in a relationship that used up her time and prevented her from doing well, and from having friends. "I learned that it's important to have a life outside of a relationship."

Kristine credits her mom for helping her get through her freshman year. "She motivates me," she says. "She helps me get through my depression. She suffers from it too. She's my backbone. She pushes me." Kristine tells me that last year when her depression reached its peak, her mom quit her job as a teacher, sold her house and moved down here to be with Kristine. Her mom bought a house, got a job and found a therapist for Kristine. They live together and Kristine is doing much better.

Kristine says that when it comes to studying she has made some changes since her freshman year. Her freshman year she reports studying thirty minutes a night, "if that." Now, in her senior year, she studies three hours a night.

Her freshman year was her easiest year in that "the professors understood we were just kids. They were more lenient. In one class I did nothing. I gave my professor my sob story; he had me memorize a poem and gave me a B for the class. In my math class I had an F. My professor gave me two tests at finals and I got an A in the class." On the other hand, her freshman year was the most difficult year because that's when her depression hit her.

Kristine says that even though she had many challenges her freshman year, she wouldn't change a thing. "I learned from everything," she says. What she'll always remember about her freshman year was being on the step team for her dorm. "It brought me out of my comfort zone. I don't like to stand out. But I did it. I stuck it out and I performed. That was fun."

Her favorite thing about being a college student is "learning about my history. Every day I learn something," she says. She wasn't a person who cared about history, even the history of African Americans. But "seeing how passionate my professors are" made her become passionate about the subject. Her professors are also something she will miss about college. "A few of them made an impact on me," she says. "I've been able to talk to them and open up."

What Kristine won't miss about college are finals, research papers, cafeteria food and having to take the train and the bus to school.

Kristine offers this advice to incoming freshmen: "If you have a problem ask yourself why you have this issue and find out ways to fix it. Seek someone older, wiser."

"Take school seriously—your freshman year dictates how you're going to do in college."

School Psychologist

Because of the stress that freshmen often experience as first-time college students, they may need to visit the school's counseling center. Dr. Bradford is a counselor here who also attended an HBCU. She says that being a school counselor was her "calling," because she "always enjoyed helping people." She especially enjoys working with college students, and she has much help and advice to offer them.

Dr. Bradford says that for freshmen, homesickness is a major problem. "They're transitioning from being under the eye of parents or guardians and are socially trying to find their place." Further, she says, freshmen are trying to find out who they can trust and figuring "out how to make new friends." The freshman year often leads to a lot of breakups, she says. Relationships with people back home often come to an end because the student is in a college far away. That's a major form of stress for freshmen. Another can develop when the student is the first in the family to attend college. "The family often doesn't know how to support the student," she says. She says that these students play a "dual role" in that they are students and are still very involved with the family back home and the problems the family may be having. This participation in the problems at home makes it difficult for the freshman to be a student. Dr. Bradford says this is a common conflict for students who attend HBCU's.

I ask Dr. Bradford if there is a difference in the type of help males and females need. "Males," she says, "usually don't come on their own. They are usually referred by judicial." Violent and aggressive behaviors are often the reasons males are referred to the counseling center. "The males are acting out," Dr. Bradford says. "They're dealing with some hurt or disappointment."

"Females are more likely to use the center," she says. "They are more likely to open up and speak about their problems." What Dr. Bradford is seeing more of today is friction between people (often females) from different regions of the country. "How people from different regions interact is a point of conflict," she says. "They might look like me but they don't act like me," is the prevailing thought. Sometimes these differences lead to fights. An example of a regional difference that students from the South have pointed out to Dr. Bradford is that they often have conflicts with students from New York, who they describe as "talking all the time." In other words, they perceive people from New York as being "pushy." What freshmen need to do, Dr. Bradford says, is learn to deal with people who were brought up differently from them.

Another geographical-based problem that freshmen may face is when they are from the suburbs or the country but attend a school in the city. A school in the heart of a major city may engender in freshmen the sense of not feeling safe, especially if the campus is open and people from the community can come in and are free to walk around.

According to Dr. Bradford, the three greatest sources of stress for freshmen are "being away from home, not being academically prepared and not knowing where to turn for help." She says the best way to deal with homesickness and feelings of not fitting in is to join groups and organizations that are centered around something the student is interested in. In the classroom, the greatest source of stress comes from a student's not being prepared for college-level work. Dr. Bradford says that "poor study skills" and "poor communication skills" are often at the heart of this problem. She says what students often fail to realize, and what exacerbates their difficulties, is that students don't know where to turn for help in the classroom. "They need to be made aware of places like the writing center and the tutoring center," she says.

To avoid stress as much as possible, freshmen not only need to use the resources available to them, but they need to work on their time management. "Avoid over-involvement in things outside the classroom," she says. "Avoid making friends too easily. Friends can disappoint; let the friendship come naturally." Finally, to avoid stress, she says students need "to monitor social media use." Students today are searching the Internet and using their phones so much that it interferes with the things that they should be doing that will benefit them in the future. She gives the example of a female senior who wants to be a lawyer but didn't take the LSAT or apply for internships because she was too busy with social media. Dr. Bradford says that students, freshmen too, should be preparing for what they will do after they graduate and shouldn't let other things get in the way.

Other advice she has for freshmen is to "get to know your professors before an issue arises." She says to make sure the professor knows your face and name and that you are someone who cares about the class. "Also," she says, "you might have to end up asking for recommendation letters from your professors," so make sure they know you.

Dr. Bradford says that freshmen should apply for internships. She hears the people in Career Services say that thousands of openings go unfilled because students don't apply for them. "Register with Career Services," she says, "and be prepared for after you graduate."

Finally, she says, "Get involved, but not too involved with the campus. Make new friends and keep some old friends. Have a good mix of old and new."

How Freshman Year Changes You

May 5

Tiara

A Mass Media major with a concentration in print journalism, Tiara is a senior from Trenton, New Jersey. "I had to go to college," she says. "There were no other options for me." Both her parents are college graduates and she knew she wanted to go. "College seemed like the place for grownups," she says. "That was where I wanted to be." After graduation, Tiara doesn't know what she's going to do. "I pray I find something good, something fulfilling," she says. "I'm leaning towards media in the entertainment industry, publishing, PR, something exciting. I want to do something I love and that excites me."

Tiara admits that she hasn't always been the best student. "I didn't realize college wasn't a game till my junior year." She says that she wasn't focused and studied very little. "I failed Biology twice." On the third try she received a D. Her current G.P.A. is 2.1. She's learned several important lessons since her freshman year. The first lesson she learned is not "to waste time. You think you have time to throw away. You don't have that. Get it done now," she says. "I'm a slacker—procrastination is my middle name." Another lesson she's learned is that she needs "to get out of my shell. I don't like to be around other people," she says. "But I learned I need to come out of my shell and poke my head around." For example, she says that she learned that she can talk to some of her professors "like a friend." Tiara cites talking to her professors as an important lesson she learned in order to be a better student, along with going to classes, doing assignments and caring about your education.

According to Tiara, her biggest challenge as a student has always been "getting to graduation." Always worried about her grades, Tiara can't quite believe she's nearing "the finish line." Two things have helped her get through college: her friends and her mom. "My friends pulled me through," she says. Her friends were always with her. "One time we had to look through our closets for old text books to sell back for money so we could eat. We've been poor together." And, if not for her mom, Tiara says, "I would have dropped out. She cares for me mentally, emotionally and financially. Mom is my backbone."

Tiara sees her freshman year as her easiest in that "Everything was fun and exciting, and scary being around people I didn't know." Her freshman year was also the most difficult year because everything was "new and exciting." She says that students come to college thinking they can become someone new, that they can change. She learned that that isn't a good idea. "Come to college and be yourself." If she could do her freshman year over again, Tiara says she would get tutors for her classes, especially Biology, Algebra and Spanish. One thing she will always remember about her freshman year is "hanging out on campus till three in the morning."

When it comes to being a college student, Tiara says her favorite things are "the freedom, making choices, and making mistakes." Another thing she enjoys is the fact that "people respect college students. They say, 'You're in school. You're doing something.'" In a lowered voice, Tiara says, "Little do they know about my grades and that I'm broke." She will miss her professors when she graduates and their "breathing down my butt all the time to get my work done." What she won't miss is "getting up for class every day and doing research."

Advice she has for incoming freshmen is to "Don't be afraid to explore—just do it.

"And please don't dress like a fool—no pajamas. You never know who's walking on campus. And guys, when you go into the classroom with your butt cheeks hanging out, what do you think your professor is thinking about you?"

Samantha

Samantha is a senior English major from Houston, Texas who began her freshman year as a Chemistry major, then switched to Biology only to later change to English. "I always knew I wanted to be an English major, but I didn't know what I would do with an English degree. I was worried about the money I would make. I was first a Science major because I thought maybe I'd be a doctor," she says. She settled on her first love, English, and plans to pursue an M.A. in English then a Ph.D. in Education Administration. She'd like to teach but sees herself eventually as a school principal.

Coming to school as a freshman, Samantha envisioned college as "fun and challenging." Both her parents attended college and gave her advice. She has to laugh at her mother's first piece of advice. "She told me not to get pregnant," Samantha says. "You better not come home pregnant, she told me. She also told me to stay focused and come home with my degree. My dad told me to stay in Texas and go to a public school so it would be cheaper," she says.

Samantha learned two important lessons her first year of college. The first was how to manage her time. "I failed a class my first semester. Failure taught me that I needed to manage my time better. I used my free time to call people, hang out in my room on the computer, just killing time. I learned to use that time to study and prepare for tests," she says. Getting a job her sophomore year helped her to structure her time and use it more wisely. The other lesson she learned her freshman year was to break away from her shyness. "I'm a shy person. I sit back and observe people. I'm afraid to open up and ask for help. I don't want to sound needy," she says. She realized that she needed help in her classes and spoke to her professors about it. Once she did that she was better able to understand what her professors expected from her.

As a member of the Honors Program, Samantha became worked up when her G.P.A. dipped to 2.4. "I cried," she says. "I asked myself, What am I doing? I knew it wasn't enough. I wasn't doing what I was capable of." A friend of hers who was on academic probation had to leave school because of her grades and this event shook Samantha. That's when she said to herself, "This is really real. I don't want to get sent home." That event, coupled with the death of her grandmother, motivated Samantha to do better. "For a week I didn't do anything, just stayed in my room after my grandmother died, then I heard her voice saying to me, 'You got to get your shit together. You fall, you get back up. Get up and walk.'"

Besides changing her approach to her classes after her freshman year, Samantha also made another change. She changed the group of people she hung out with. She hung out with a group of friends she describes as "messy, flamboyant, mediocre students." One night in Samantha's room they were smoking something they shouldn't have been smoking in a dorm room. The RA came in the room and asked who was responsible and her friends pointed at her. That's when she realized she needed new friends.

Her freshman year was her easiest year because she had morning classes. "I hate afternoon classes," she says. "I have a hard time concentrating after a certain point." Her freshman year was her most difficult year because she had to "adjust to being away from home. I didn't have a car, had to share space with a roommate. I'm an only child. I'm not used to sharing a room. I had problems with privacy issues."

The one thing she would do differently if she could do her freshman year over would be to come to school as an English major. "I wouldn't think about money," she says. "I would've taken school more seriously." The one thing she will always remember about her freshman year is "being inducted into the Honors Program. They helped me all the time," she says. "I would ask them how to handle situations and they would tell me."

Samantha says the best thing about being a college student is that it "keeps me motivated, keeps me on my toes, organized and structured." She says, "It gives me a sense of purpose." What she'll miss about college is the prestige she says being a college student gives her. When I ask her what she won't miss, she can't come up with anything. She says, "I love school. I've always had a passion for education. I love learning and applying it to my everyday life. Last week I went to Mexico for Spring break. I was speaking Spanish in Mexico!" she says with a proud look on her face.

Her advice to freshmen is to "take advantage of the time you have. If you need to study more, use that time to study more. Use that time to do what you need to do."

Tameka

Tameka has taken most of her finals (she already knows she got an A in history) and is planning her summer. She's worked her last day at Walmart. I ask if she'll go back come August. "We'll see," she says. "My manager said, 'You better come back.' She knows I'm dependable, on time and I work hard." Next week at home she has an interview at SHEETZ for a summer job that pays more than her usual job at Bojangle's. On Tuesdays and Thursdays she will be shadowing her dentist to get a feel for her future profession. And, also, she'll be taking two classes at the community college.

Even though Tameka left her return to Walmart up in the air with the manager, she is doubtful that she will go back in the fall. She is going to be an RA and will have her hands full with that responsibility. She's hoping for the job at SHEETZ this summer so that she can save up and live off that money while she's in school. That way she won't have to work at Walmart. Being an RA will help Tameka financially since she won't have to pay for her room and board next year.

This is our last meeting so it's time to assess her freshman year. I first ask her how her second semester was different from her first. "I was more prepared for the second semester but less focused. I was waiting to start my life at work; working gives my life structure. I don't like being without a job. I do better with my time when I have a job."

What ideas you had about college have changed? "Nothing really. I just hate finals and boring teachers. But that's life."

What ideas about yourself have changed? "The classes you worry about the most, you do the best in."

What was your biggest success your freshman year? "Working and doing well in school and getting the RA position."

What was your biggest disappointment? "If I don't get all A's, that will be my biggest disappointment."

What are the most important lessons you learned your freshman year? "You got to do what you got to do to get your way." I ask her if her background—coming from a single-parent household where she's always needed to work—plays a role in the way she approaches her responsibilities. "I wouldn't work as hard if I had money," she says. "My background pushes me to do better in school."

What have you learned about your fellow college students? "Not everybody comes to college for the right reason. Some come to get away from home or just because they were accepted. That affects their grades."

What have you learned about college life? "You can't socialize, sleep and study all at the same time. You got to pick two—two at a time. Sometimes I sacrificed socializing, sometimes sleep and sometimes studying." She also says, "You need to choose your professors wisely. I should've known better when there were no comments about my World Lit. instructor on ratemyprofessor.com. I won't make that mistake again."

What will you tell your children about your freshman year? "I'm going to tell them to pay attention to who they room with because they might end up rooming with a monster. That's what happened to me. I'll tell them I performed well my freshman year because I remembered why I was in school. That's what they'll need to know."

If you could address this fall's incoming freshman class, what would you tell them? "If you're taking a full load, like eighteen credits for a semester, take it in the fall, not the spring. College students are more focused in the fall than the spring. Your mind wanders in the spring when the weather gets warmer."

"Meet with your professors, especially if you aren't doing well in the class."

"Time management is the key to college life."

"Don't get dumb friends. If you have dumb friends and they're supposed to work with you on a group project, tell them you can't work with them. Make friends who are smart and who have a good work ethic. Look for friends who are older and who give you good advice."

Ashley

Squeezed for time, I need to rush through the last interview with Ashley, which isn't something I want to do. I look forward to talking to Ashley and Tameka and hearing about what is going on in their lives. I like to spend time with them.

Despite the fact that it is twelve thirty in the afternoon Ashley comes to my office looking very tired. "I just woke up," she says. It's finals week and she's been up late studying. In fact she had taken a final this morning in her English class, the class in which nothing had been required, until, that is, the very end of the semester. They took their exit exam, took a final and had to turn in a literary analysis that served as their research paper.

Two weeks ago Ashley attended the Freshman Awards. I ask her if she won anything. Still sleepy, she looks confused at my question. I try again. "What?" she says. I explain how she'd told me she'd been invited and told me she had to go, but that she didn't know what she would win. "Did you win?" I ask. "Yeah, something," she says. "I can't remember, honor roll or Dean's List. I don't know." I laugh. "Could it be both?" I say. "Maybe. I don't know," she replies.

I wake her up when I ask her if she'll be an RA next year. Her head, which had been drooping, shoots up and her face lights up. "I got it," she says, smiling. "I'm going to be an RA." I ask about it. "I get free room and board and a book scholarship." I ask how much the book scholarship is. "I have no idea," she says. The one negative aspect of Ashley's assignment as an RA is that she won't be rooming with her best friend next year. She tells me that her roommate will be living with other people from the hall.

I move to the reflective questions about her freshman year. How was this semester different from the first? "It's better," she says. "I met more people. There was a lot more going on this semester. I was always doing something. I wasn't always in my room sleeping like last semester."

What ideas you had about college have changed? "That college is hard. It's not that hard." She is quick to qualify—"If you study it's not too hard." I ask her about her ideas concerning partying. When we first met she said she thought she'd do a lot of partying. "I only partied about twice a month," she says. "I'm a work-first type of person."

Building on that, she says, "I'm no party child. I've come to the realization that I'm a nerd. I always thought I was someone who just did my work, but I'm a nerd. I take my education very seriously. Thursday I was up until three studying and Sunday till five. I'm determined to get a 4.0, not this semester, but eventually." She reports that she did change her major from Education to Math.

What was your biggest success your freshman year? "Not quitting, being able to bounce back. I didn't get to be an orientation guide, but I got to be an RA, which is better, more benefits."

What was your biggest disappointment? She looks up in the air, considering. She makes a humming noise. "I don't think I have one," she says. Then she adds, "The food still sucks. I run through so much money on food" to avoid eating at the school's cafeteria.

What are the most important lessons you learned your freshman year? "Everything happens in time. Last semester I had friends. This semester I have real friends, friends I can count on, who mean something to me."

What have you learned about your fellow college students? Repeating something she's told me before, she replies, "That you can still pass even if you don't come to class. There was a guy in my math class last semester who never came to class and he's in my math class this semester. You had to pass last semester to be in the class this semester, which means he must have passed somehow."

Years from now, what will you tell your children about your freshman year? "That it was peculiar, yet fun. No one can tell you what your freshman year is going to be. You have to experience it yourself."

If you could address this fall's incoming freshman class, what would you tell them? "Be ready to learn in all aspects, in the classroom, about yourself, your professors, people around you, your surroundings. You will learn a lot. Be ready to learn."

Reggie

Here is the last update from Reggie:

"My final grades were a C in College Algebra, a B in Art and Speech and an A in College Comp II. I'm content with them, although I wish my B's were A's and I had a 3.2 instead of a 3.0.

The best thing that happened to me this semester was not having financial aid issues at my new school. The worst thing that happened was having to leave [our school]. My freshmen year has changed my outlook on life and my thought process. I feel more mature and "grown-up" because I had to handle all my college business on my own. I will be going back to [my present school] for the fall and hopefully [return to our school] in the spring. Because I'm trying to improve my GPA as much as possible to get scholarships to go back to [our school].

I actually spoke with the family [he stayed with here] last week and they're coming to visit next month. I talk to the oldest son on the phone sometimes, although he can't really talk. I talk to the wife maybe once a month [;] we get along a lot better not living together. They called me to help dress their middle son for prom because their fashion sense is 0. My mom speaks with them occasionally too [. . .]."

FINAL GRADES

On the left are the predicted grades. On the right are the earned grades.

Tameka

	Grade predicted	Grade earned
Critical Thinking	A	A
History	A	A
Biology II	A	A
Pre-calculus	A	A
First-Year Seminar	A	A
French	A	W

Ashley

Biology	A	B
First-Year Seminar	A	A
Calculus I	A	A
Pre-calculus II	A	A
Speech	A	A
English	A	B

Freshman Year G.P.A.

Tameka	4.0
Ashley	3.72

Afterword

The freshman year is over for Tameka, Michael, Ashley and Reggie. It has unfolded before our eyes and has revealed itself to be everything people say it is—challenging, unpredictable, stressful, exciting, fun. Through Tameka's experience we see the benefits of remaining focused on a goal and doing what is needed to attain that goal. Michael's story is one of unquestioned enthusiasm mixed with the harsh reality of the demands of the college classroom, as well as the demands of economics. Ashley's even-tempered, steady approach to all aspects of her life reveal a young woman whose stable background helped to create a well-balanced student. Lastly, Reggie's story can be seen as a cautionary tale about coming to college without making sure everything is in place before beginning what has the potential to be one of the most difficult times in a student's life.

From the students interviewed, as well as from the faculty and staff featured in this book, several repeating themes emerge. The first is that students cannot be prepared enough intellectually and financially for what college demands. Second, when students lose their focus on academics and let themselves be distracted, their grades become a casualty, and if there is any lesson to learn from these pages, it is that getting poor grades is easy to do and that maintaining good grades requires strict attention and dedication. Third, no one knows what will happen while in college, and students, who are able to adjust without losing focus on why they are in college, usually persevere. Finally, the college experience can be one of the most rewarding and enriching experiences in a person's life, but only if that person believes in what he or she is doing and has a plan to accomplish that goal. When that isn't the case, money is wasted and dreams dashed.

While I had ideas about what freshmen would tell me concerning their first year of college, I learned from them that there are many things I didn't know about freshmen and the freshman experience. It is my hope that readers also have learned from these students what being a freshman at an HBCU encompasses as well as what it requires. Ultimately, what I hope readers take away from the students profiled in this book is that in order to succeed in anything—but especially in college—people need to learn from each other. When we learn the lessons those who have gone before us have to teach, we become educated.

Works Cited

"Black Students' College Graduation Rates Remain Low, but Modest Progress Begins to Show." 2006. The Journal of Blacks in Higher Education. 6 Sept. 2013. Web.

"College Students: Getting Enough Sleep is Vital to Academic Success." 30 Nov. 2007. American Academy of Sleep Medicine. 11 Sept. 2013. Web.

Dell-Antonia, KJ. "The Link Between Reading Level and Dropout Rates." 19 March 2012. The New York Times. 9 Sept. 2013. Web.

Levitt, Steven D. and Stephen J. Dubner. Freakonomics. New York: Harper Perennial. 2009. Print.

Sullivan, Bob. "Students can't resist distraction for two minutes . . . and neither can you." 18 May 2103. NBC News: Technology. 25 Nov. 2013. Web.

"Sleep Disorders Health Center." WebMD. 11 Sept. 2013. Web.

X, Malcolm. The Autobiography of Malcolm X. New York: Grove Press. 1966. Print.